FIRST-YEAR GUITAR
Third Edition

A Classroom Text

by

NANCY LEE MARSTERS

This text is dedicated to the guitar students, past and present, of

Leon High School

Tallahassee, Florida

Essential support was provided by those listed below, to whom I offer my deepest thanks.

Cover: Philip and Nancy Lynn Morales

Photos: Scott Brouwer

Drawings: Chris Hobgood and Philip Morales

Technical Advisor, Model: Leo Welch

Computer Consultant: Portia Thomas

Editors: Jon and Judy Arthur, Claudia Dew, Ray Kickliter, Julia Price, Leo Welch

The materials in this book are, to the best of my
knowledge, either new and original applications
or existent in the public domain. Musical
examples not bearing credits are of
my own invention.

TABLE OF CONTENTS

(Roots)

INDEX OF SONGS (lead sheets)

PREFACE

To the Student:

This is an introductory course designed to help you learn many of the different styles and techniques of guitar playing. Each unit includes many playing activities and written exercises which are essential to the playing section. The written portions are not busy work. Please make a strong effort to UNDERSTAND all parts of all units, written and played, as they build upon each other. What you learn in each unit will be useful later in the course.

Your progress in guitar playing is almost totally dependent upon you. Although most people think that music educators are hired to teach students to sing or to play instruments, what we really do is teach students how to train themselves. In the final analysis, the real music educator is YOU. YOU absorb the instruction, YOU systematically apply it to practice patterns, YOU discipline your fingers. No one else can accomplish progress for you. It's been my experience that the best players at the end of each year are not necessarily those who are the smartest or those who have been blessed with the best physical coordination. The finest players, year after year, have been those who really worked at it, those who were committed to playing well. With a positive attitude and a firm end goal in mind, these students created a self-discipline for practice which rewarded them, ultimately, with fine playing skills. I hope that each of you is one of these disciplined people and that this book will help you to reach the playing goals you've set for yourself.

To the Teacher:

In each unit, basic concepts are taught first to the entire group. Usually, motor skills precede all other training. Then, each student works at his/her own pace, but within teacher-defined deadlines. Definitive strategies and timelines for instruction, written and played testing procedures, examinations for all units and day-by-day lesson plans may be found in the available teacher manual. THE METHOD IS MORE IMPORTANT THAN THE MATERIALS.

Every lesson contained here has been field-tested in several classrooms and, if followed carefully, will lead to student success. Though the text was developed in, and is specifically designed for the secondary school classroom, it may be used effectively for private teaching and college level courses as well.

It should be emphasized that this is a text, not a text and songbook. It contains a systematic introduction to the basic tools of good guitar playing and simple examples for each technique. Enough music has been included for this task, BUT NO MORE, keeping the cost as low as possible so you will be able to purchase the variety of music materials your students LIKE AND NEED. Supplementary song volumes containing current pop, rock, country and general styles are available from many publishers. These books, often labeled "easy guitar", use simple key signatures and rhythmic notation designed for the beginner. As soon as a technique is learned through the text, the student may apply it immediately to favorite tunes. The result is a strong motivation for disciplined practice, leading to quicker playing progress.

INTRODUCTORY UNIT

POSITIONING THE BODY FOR PLAYING

Playing positions may vary with the type of guitar played. This text uses the classical position for the beginning student as it can be successfully applied to the playing of folk, rock, jazz and classical styles. Note the pictures here. The player is seated on the FRONT EDGE of the chair. The left leg is

positioned on a small footstool. The footstool is available at your music store—or you might want to construct your own. The guitar is placed on the left thigh. Each player should adjust the footstool so

that the head of the instrument is about at eye level. The right leg is placed in such a way that the bottom right edge of the guitar body can rest on it. Placement of this leg varies with the height of the individual player and the chair on which the player sits. The upper back edge of the guitar body rests on the chest. This position leaves almost the entire back of the instrument body free to vibrate.

PLACING THE LEFT HAND

A good left hand position is critical to fine playing. It is very important that each student develop a good position at the BEGINNING stages of study. Start by placing the thumb as shown in the picture at left below. Next, add the fingers by placing them on the fingerboard as shown in the picture at

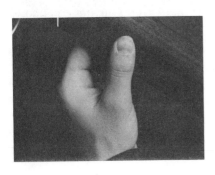

right. Notice that the thumb is **not** bent at the first knuckle and that each finger is **curved** so that only the **tips** touch the

guitar fretboard. Practice holding the instrument with each finger in a different fret and the thumb positioned about between the index and middle fingers. Avoid "strangling" the neck of the guitar as this will impede movement of your left hand as you expand your playing skills.

PLACING THE RIGHT HAND

This picture indicates the positioning of the right arm and hand. This placement will allow the player proper use of the hand and fingers in all applications in this text.

Beginning players may choose to strum with the thumb or pick. It is recommended that you learn both. TO STRUM WITH THE THUMB, simply move the hand from the wrist and elbow so that the thumb passes evenly over ALL the strings. The motion is much like what you would do to shake water off your fingers. Though there will be some chords which require you to avoid strumming one or two low strings, it is very important that the strum include ALL UPPER STRINGS. (Upper strings are those closest to your feet.)

TO STRUM WITH THE PICK, place the right arm in the regular position. Hold the pick between the thumb and index finger as shown in these pictures. Move the right hand as when strumming with the thumb. Once again, be sure the pick is strumming all the upper strings. Further instructions on use of the right hand are in the sections of this book which deal with playing scales and arpeggios.

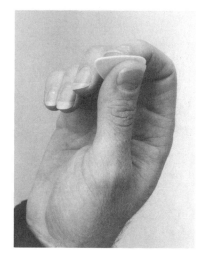

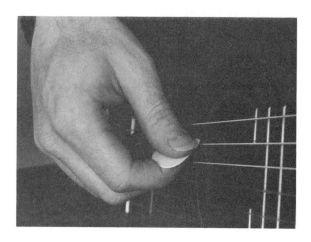

INTRODUCTION TO THE GUITAR

There are many types of guitars, including classical, folk and electric models. Construction varies among them, but the basic principles of playing have much in common. The student who learns to play on one type of instrument will have little difficulty playing the other types.

Below is a drawing of a classical guitar with its parts labeled.

MEMORIZE THE PARTS OF THIS GUITAR.

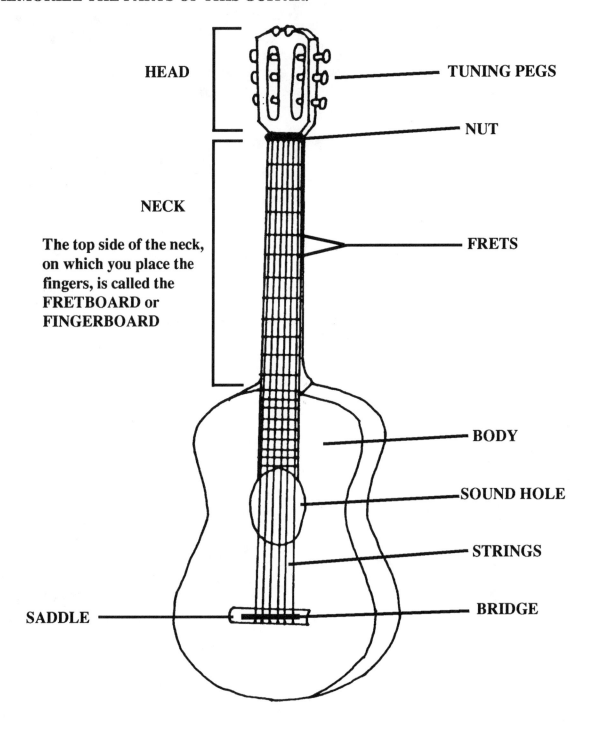

HEAD

TUNING PEGS

NUT

NECK

The top side of the neck, on which you place the fingers, is called the FRETBOARD or FINGERBOARD

FRETS

BODY

SOUND HOLE

STRINGS

SADDLE

BRIDGE

TUNING THE GUITAR

Tuning a guitar is an exercise in ear training. Over a period of time you will learn to identify whether the string you are tuning is higher, lower or the same as your reference pitch. IT IS VERY IMPORTANT TO BE PATIENT WITH YOURSELF as you approach this task. Take your time with each string and listen carefully. Good tuning skills come gradually and shouldn't be rushed.

The figure at left below shows how to tune a guitar to the piano. Note that the guitar sounds a full octave below the notated pitches. The figure at right below shows the letter names of the six numbered guitar strings. **MEMORIZE THEM.**

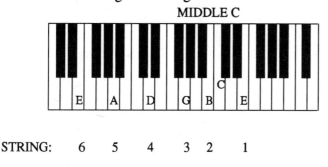

STRING: 6   5   4   3   2   1

Figure 1

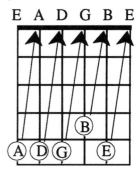

STRING: 6 5 4 3 2 1

Figure 2

Learn to tune the guitar to itself.

1) Begin with the 6th string (E). Tune this string to the piano, tuning fork, pitchpipe or other device. Tighten the string to raise the pitch; loosen it to lower the pitch.
2) Next, place your finger on the 5th fret of string 6. **Play this string only.** Match the pitch of the open string 5 (A) to the note you just played on string 6 (A), as shown in Figure 3.
3) Once you have matched the 5th string to the "A" sound taken from string 6, proceed to tune the other strings in a similar manner.
4) Find the "D" pitch on the 5th fret of string 5 (figure 4). Tune string 4.
5) Find the "G" pitch on the 5th fret of string 4 (figure 5). Tune string 3.
6) Find the "B" pitch on the **4th fret** of string 3 (figure 5). Tune string 2.
7) Find the high "E" on the 5th fret of string 2 (figure 5). Tune string 1.

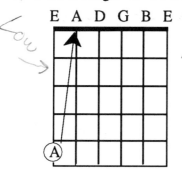

Figure 3

Figure 4

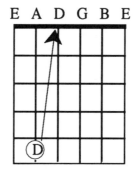

Figure 5

UNIT ONE

PLAYING RHYTHM GUITAR

The guitar can be played as a rhythm instrument, a melody instrument, or a combination of the two. Your first lessons are in rhythm guitar. The goal is to master several chords in order to provide strumming accompaniment to melody. Remember, in this segment you are not playing the melody. That comes later.

THE LEFT HAND FINGERS

Figure 6 shows the numbers assigned to the fingers of your left hand. Notice that the thumb is not numbered. **MEMORIZE THE FINGER NUMBERS.**

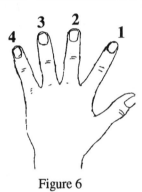

Figure 6

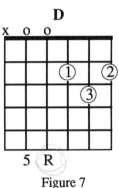

Figure 7

THE CHORD DIAGRAM

The chord diagram is a representation of the guitar fingerboard. Look at figure 7. Notice these important features:

1) The strings are represented from the lowest in pitch to the highest (lowest string is on the left of the diagram).
2) The nut is at the upper edge of the diagram with the frets arranged below it.
3) Numbers show left hand finger placement.
4) "o" shows an open string, a string on which no finger is placed. **Strum open strings.**
5) "x" shows an unplayed string. **Avoid strumming this string.**
6) Chords in Unit One contain at least three pitches: root (R), third and fifth (5). The ROOT is the basis of the chord and carries the chord's letter name. The root of all D chords (such as D, Dm, D7) is D, and is labeled above with an "R" below string 4 (the D string). The fifth of the D chord is found on string 5, labeled above with a "5" below the 5th string. Both R (root) and 5 (fifth) of each chord in Unit One will be used in strumming patterns. **MEMORIZE THEM AS YOU PROCEED THROUGH THE UNIT.**
7) In Figure 7, the D chord, your first finger is placed on string 3 at the second fret, your second finger on string 1 at the second fret and your third finger on string 2 at the third fret. Strings 4 and 5 are strummed open (o) and string 6 is NOT STRUMMED (x).

PLAY THE "D" CHORD.

MUSIC TERMS USED IN THIS UNIT

CHORD: three or more pitches played at once (block chord) or one after another (arpeggio)

PROGRESSION: a series of chords

SCALE: an organized series of notes, arranged in stepwise order

KEY: indicates the name of the FIRST NOTE OF THE SCALE on which the music is based.

I - IV - V7: a PROGRESSION using chords built upon pitches I, IV and V of the scale. Chord I always carries the letter name of the KEY, the first note of the scale.

"GUIDE", "COMMON" AND "RELATIVE" FINGERS

When moving from one chord to another, you will find COMMON, GUIDE and RELATIVE fingers to help you to change smoothly. Fingerings given in this section are suggested for beginners. Some alternate fingerings, however, are provided.

COMMON fingers are those which are in **exactly the same position** for both chords involved in a change.

GUIDE fingers are those which **remain on a string but move to a new fret** when changing from one chord to another.

RELATIVE fingers are those which are **related by position** in both chords involved in a change.

E - Z MOVER

In this unit you will find **E-Z MOVER** diagrams to help you shift easily from one chord to another. These diagrams, enclosed in a box such as the one shown above, accompany the introduction of each new progression.

MEMORIZE ALL TERMS ON THIS PAGE.

THE "D" PROGRESSION

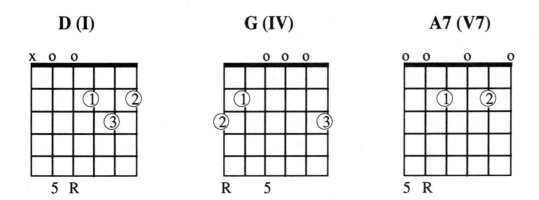

D (I) **G (IV)** **A7 (V7)**

In this unit, you will learn a **I-IV-V7** progression in each key. For the key of D, those chords are D-G-A7. To change easily from D to A7, move fingers 1 and 2 AT THE SAME TIME. Notice that they are in the same **RELATIVE** position for both chords (figure 8).

In changing from D to G, finger 3 is **RELATIVE**, as shown in figure 9. Place this finger first, then place fingers 1 and 2. Eventually, all fingers will move together.

Changing from G to A7, finger 1 is **RELATIVE**; move it to the adjacent string, then place finger 2 (figure 10).

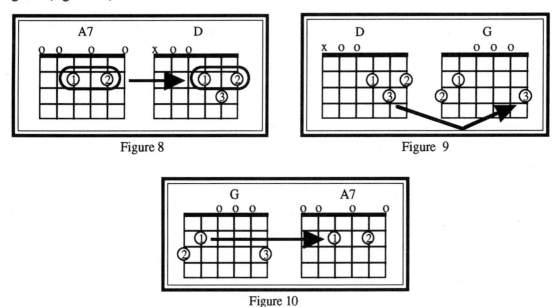

Figure 8   Figure 9

Figure 10

PRACTICE PROCEDURES:

1) Strum with DOWN STROKES unless instructed otherwise.
2) Practice moving between two chords at a time. Begin with D and A7, strumming each chord 8 times. Then try it with 6 strums, then with 4, 2 and 1.

Move on to the next page to learn how to apply these chords to songs.

READING THE RHYTHM GUITAR PART IN MUSIC

Guitar music is written on a **STAFF**, which has 5 lines and 4 spaces.

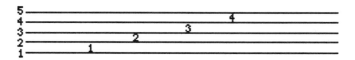

At the beginning of each staff of guitar music you will see the **TREBLE (G) CLEF.**

Each line of music has perpendicular lines, known as **BAR LINES,** which divide the music into **MEASURES.** The **DOUBLE BAR LINE** always indicates the end of the music and is sometimes used to separate sections of a piece.

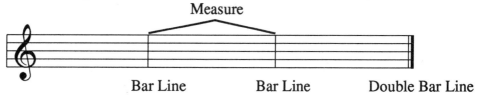

The two numbers following the **TREBLE CLEF** constitute the **TIME SIGNATURE.** For this unit, you only need to understand the TOP NUMBER of the time signature. It tells you HOW MANY BEATS ARE IN EACH MEASURE. At this point, you should strum once for each beat.

In the example below, the time signature tells you that there are 3 beats in each measure When you strum these beats, the strum must be VERY STEADY, with all beats receiving equal time.

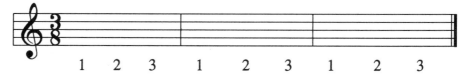

Below is a portion of the first line of "Buffalo Gals". Notice that there are 4 measures in this line and that each measure contains 4 beats. You will now find that the name of the chord to be strummed is placed above the measures. In this song, the D chord is strummed for the first 2 measures, then A7 is strummed for 1 measure and D for the final measure. (The two symbols between the clef and time signatures will be explained at a later time. Don't worry about them now.)

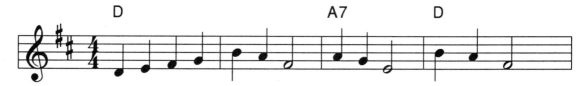

10

NOTE: The space between the time signature and the first bar line may contain a full measure or a partial one. Two of the songs below begin with a partial measure. Start strumming in the measure where you see the chord name.

SKIP TO MY LOU

Choose your part - ner, skip to my Lou. Choose your part - ner, skip to my Lou.

Choose your part - ner, skip to my Lou. Skip to my Lou, my dar - ling.

HE'S GOT THE WHOLE WORLD IN HIS HANDS

He's got the whole world—— in His hands.— He's got the whole world——

in His hands.– He's got the whole world—— in His hands.—He's got the whole world in His hands.

$\colon\|$ = *Repeat*

OH, HOW HE LIED

There was an old fel-low who smoked a ci - gar, smoked a ci - gar, smoked a ci -

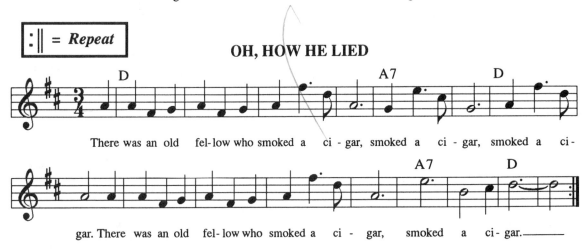

gar. There was an old fel-low who smoked a ci - gar, smoked a ci - gar.———

2. There was a young lady who played a guitar,
Played a guitar, played a guitar.
There was a young lady who played a guitar,
Played a guitar.

3. He told her he loved her but oh, how he lied,
Oh, how he lied; oh, how he lied.
He told her he loved her but oh, how he lied,
Oh, how he lied.

WHEN YOU CAN PLAY THESE SONGS, GO TO PAGE 8 AND PRACTICE:
1) D - G, 2) G - A7, 3) D - G - A7. Then play the songs on page 11.

FINE (fee-nay)	= the end
D. C. AL FINE	= go back to the beginning and play to Fine
TACET	= do not play
C	= 4/4 time (also called "common time")

MICHAEL, ROW THE BOAT ASHORE

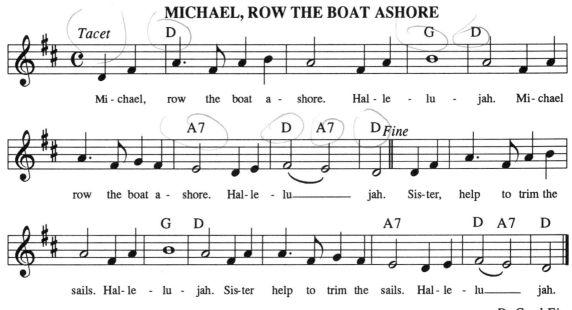

Mi - chael, row the boat a - shore. Hal - le - lu - jah. Mi - chael

row the boat a - shore. Hal - le - lu————— jah. Sis - ter, help to trim the

sails. Hal - le - lu - jah. Sis-ter help to trim the sails. Hal - le - lu————— jah.

D. C. al Fine

OH, SUSANNAH

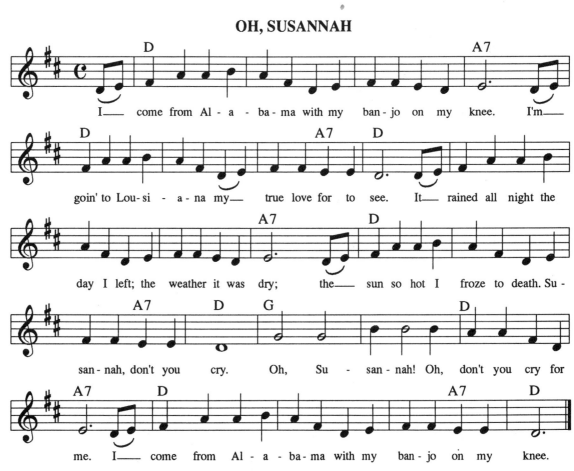

I—— come from Al - a - ba - ma with my ban - jo on my knee. I'm——

goin' to Lou - si - a - na my—— true love for to see. It—— rained all night the

day I left; the weather it was dry; the—— sun so hot I froze to death. Su -

san - nah, don't you cry. Oh, Su - san - nah! Oh, don't you cry for

me. I—— come from Al - a - ba - ma with my ban - jo on my knee.

THE "A" PROGRESSION

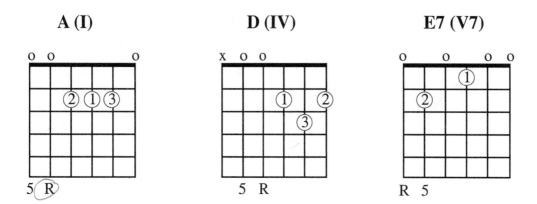

In changing from A to D, finger 1 is **COMMON.** Move as shown below, pivoting the hand on finger 1 WITHOUT moving it from its position on fret 2 (figure 11).

To change from A to E7, or from D to E7, use finger 1 as a **GUIDE.** Slide it from fret 2 to fret 1, as shown (keep the finger in contact with the string) and place the remaining finger in the correct position (figures 12 and 13).

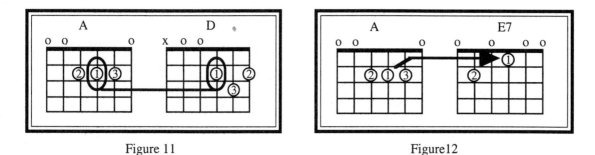

Figure 11   Figure12

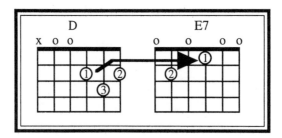

Figure 13

LEARN TO PLAY THE FOLLOWING PATTERNS SMOOTHLY:

1) A - D, 2) A - E7, 3) D - E7, 4) A - D - E7.

Once you are ready, play songs in the key of A, page 94.

THE "G" PROGRESSION

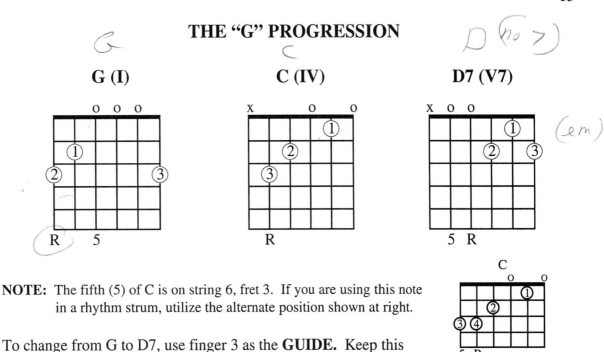

G (I) **C (IV)** **D7 (V7)**

NOTE: The fifth (5) of C is on string 6, fret 3. If you are using this note in a rhythm strum, utilize the alternate position shown at right.

To change from G to D7, use finger 3 as the **GUIDE.** Keep this finger in contact with string l as you move between these chords (figure 14). Move fingers 1 and 2 together. Changing from C to D7, finger l is **COMMON.** Pivot on this finger during the change (figure 15).

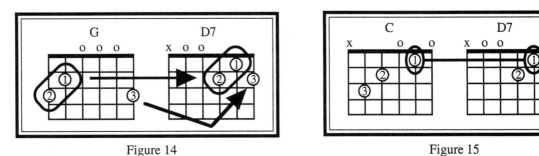

Figure 14   Figure 15

There are no common, guide or relative fingers to help in moving between C and this fingering for G. However, if you have elected to use the alternate fingering for G (figures 16-17) rather than the one above, you will find fingers 2 and 3 in a relative position to C. Guitar teachers are divided as to which G position is best for the beginning player. There are good reasons for either choice. We use the one above because it makes an easy change to D7 and delays the use of finger 4 until a later time.

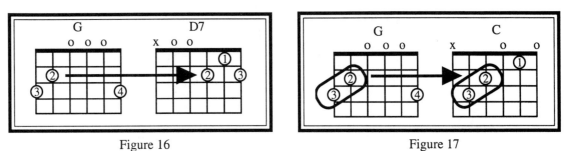

Figure 16   Figure 17

PRACTICE PROGRESSIONS: 1) C - D7, 2) D7 - G, 3) G - C, 4) G - C - D7

Play songs in the key of G, page 95.

THE "E" PROGRESSION

E (I)
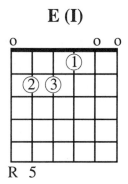

R 5

A (IV)
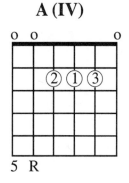

5 R

B7 (V7)
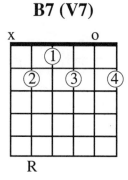

R

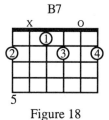

Figure 18

NOTE: The fifth (5) of B7 is found on string 6, fret 2. To play this note SINGLY, move finger 2 from string 5 across to the position shown at right. Avoid strumming string 5 (figure 18).

To change from E to A, use finger 1 as the **GUIDE.** Be sure to keep it in contact with string 3 as you move (figure 19).

Moving from E to B7, finger 2 is **COMMON.** Just leave it where it is as you change chords (figure 20).

Move from A to B7 as shown in figure 21. Fingers 2 and 3 are **RELATIVE.**

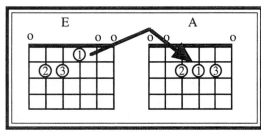

Figure 19

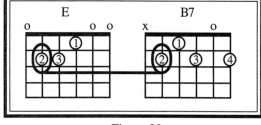

Figure 20

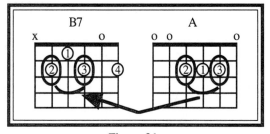

Figure 21

PRACTICE PROGRESSIONS: 1) E - A,   2) E - B7,   3) A - B7,   4) E - A - B7

Now you can play songs in the key of E, page 96, or play the 12-bar blues on pages 81-83.

THE "Em" PROGRESSION

Em (i)	Am (iv)	B7 (V7)
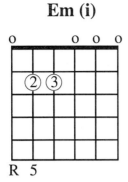	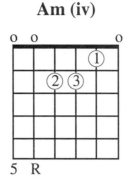	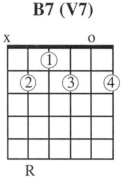

NOTE: The small "m" stands for **MINOR.** For minor chords, a lower case Roman numeral is used in writing the progression: i - iv- V7.

Moving from Em to Am, fingers 2 and 3 are in **RELATIVE** position. Always move them together (figure 22).

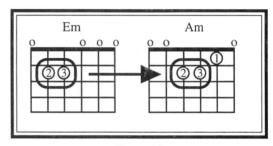

Figure 22

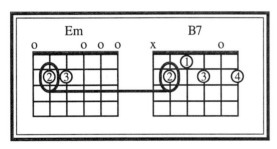

Figure 23

Moving from Em to B7, finger 2 is **COMMON** (figure 23).

Moving from Am to B7, finger 3 is **COMMON** (figure 24).

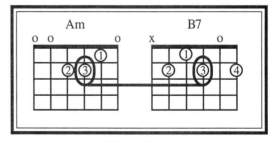

Figure 24

PRACTICE PROGRESSIONS: 1) Em - Am, 2) Am - B7, 3) Em - B7, 4) Em - Am - B7

Play songs in Em on pages 97 and 98.

THE "Am" PROGRESSION

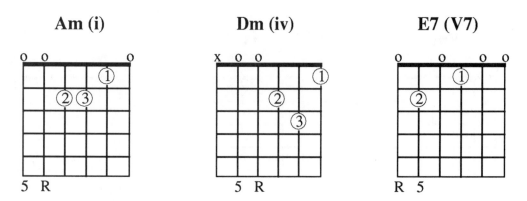

Am (i)   Dm (iv)   E7 (V7)

Fingers 1 and 2 are **RELATIVE** in all changes. Note that they stay in the same relative position for all three chords. ALWAYS MOVE THEM TOGETHER (figures 25-27). (The black dots represent third finger placement.)

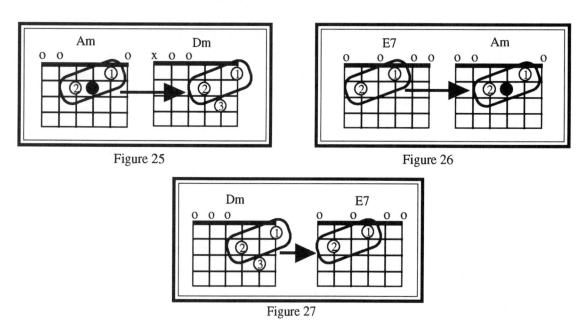

Figure 25   Figure 26

Figure 27

PRACTICE PROGRESSIONS: 1) Am - Dm,   2) Am - E7,   3) Dm - E7,
                                4) Am - Dm - E7

Play "*Song of the Volga Boatmen*" to practice the ***Am-Dm*** change.

Yo— heave ho.   Yo— heave ho.   Pull to - ge - ther.   For- ward still we go.

Play the songs in the key of Am on pages 100 and 101.

THE "C" PROGRESSION

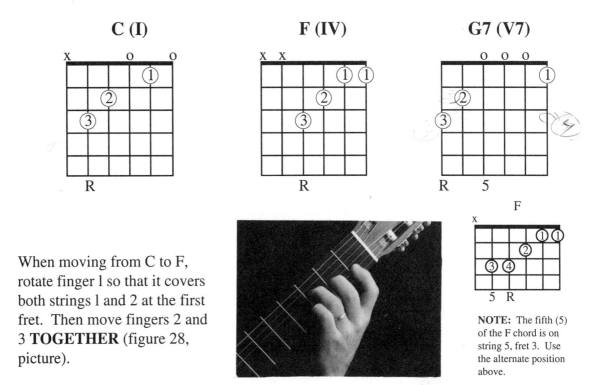

C (I)   **F (IV)**   **G7 (V7)**

When moving from C to F, rotate finger 1 so that it covers both strings 1 and 2 at the first fret. Then move fingers 2 and 3 **TOGETHER** (figure 28, picture).

F

NOTE: The fifth (5) of the F chord is on string 5, fret 3. Use the alternate position above.

Fingers 2 and 3 are in **RELATIVE** position for each chord and always move together (figures 28-30).

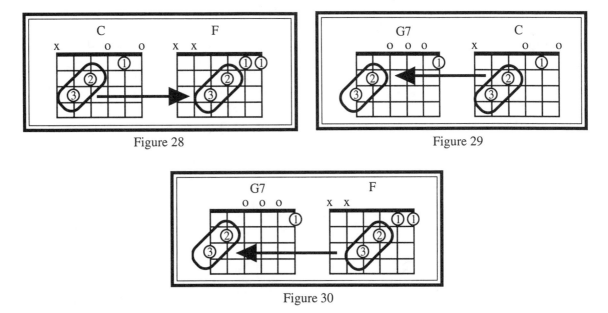

Figure 28   Figure 29

Figure 30

PRACTICE PROGRESSIONS: 1) C - F,   2) C - G7,   3) F - G7,   4) C - F - G7

Play songs in the key of C, pages 101-103.

YOU CAN NOW PLAY ANY LEAD SHEET IN THE MUSIC SECTION OF THIS TEXT. YOU WILL ALSO BE ABLE TO PLAY MANY SONGS FROM OTHER BOOKS.

APPLYING NEW STRUMMING PATTERNS TO PROGRESSIONS

When you have mastered the ability to change chords smoothly using the straight strum, you may then apply the following patterns to your rhythm accompaniment.

THE ROOT-STRUM PATTERN

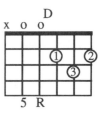

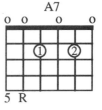

In this pattern you will simply REPLACE the first strum of each measure with the playing of the ROOT STRING ONLY. You will find these strings labeled with "R" on each chord diagram. The diagrams at right show that the ROOT STRING (R) for the D chord is string 4 and the ROOT STRING (R) for the A7 chord is string 5. When you play the root string alone, with either the right thumb or the pick, use the REST STROKE. To execute this stroke, the pick or thumb simply plays through the designated string and comes to REST on the next string. Imitate carefully the examples given in the pictures below.

REST STROKE WITH THE THUMB

Before playing string 5   *After playing string 5*

REST STROKE WITH THE PICK

Before playing string 5   *After playing string 5*

Below is a sample rhythm guitar part using only strums.   / = one strum

```
        D                              A7
  4  / / / /  / / / /  / / / /  / / / /
1 4  1 2 3 4  1 2 3 4  1 2 3 4  1 2 3 4
```

Here is the same line, but the strum appearing on the FIRST BEAT OF EACH MEASURE has been replaced with the playing of the ROOT STRING (R) of the given chord. Play both examples, imitating the technique pictures (page 18) carefully. Remember, the root string for "D" is string 4; the root string for "A7" is string 5.

```
        D                              A7
  4  R / / /  R / / /  R / / /  R / / /
2 4  1 2 3 4  1 2 3 4  1 2 3 4  1 2 3 4
```

Try playing "Skip to my Lou" (page 10) using the new pattern.

USING THE ROOT-FIFTH PATTERN

Now try a new pattern in which you play the ROOT (R) on beat 1 of each measure and the FIFTH (5) on beat 3. Review the chord diagrams on page 18 before beginning.

```
        D                              A7
  4  R / 5 /  R / 5 /  R / 5 /  R / 5 /
3 4  1 2 3 4  1 2 3 4  1 2 3 4  1 2 3 4
```

Apply the root-fifth pattern to "Skip to My Lou".

Example 4 demonstrates one way to use the root-fifth pattern in 3/4 time. Learn the pattern and then apply it to "Oh, How He Lied" (below).

```
        D                                              A7
  3  R / /  5 / /  R / /  5 / /  R / /  5 / /
4 4  1 2 3  1 2 3  1 2 3  1 2 3  1 2 3  1 2 3
```

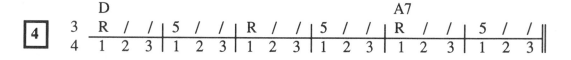

There was an old fel-low who smoked a ci - gar, smoked a ci - gar, smoked a ci-

gar. There was an old fel-low who smoked a ci - gar, smoked a ci - gar._____

REFERENCE PAGES FOR CHORD PROGRESSIONS IN UNIT ONE

KEY	I	IV	V7

D

D (I)

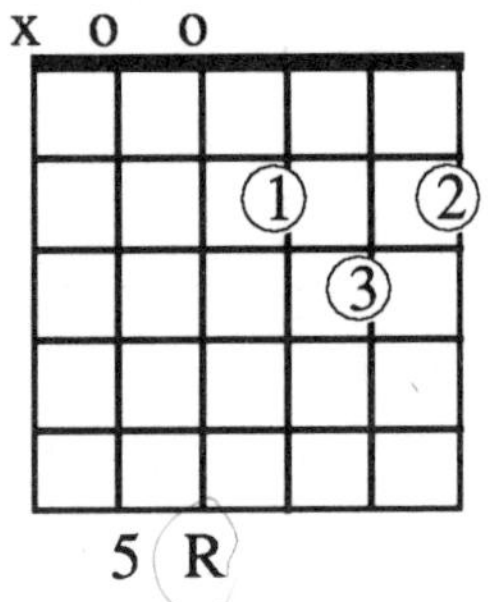

5 R

G (IV)

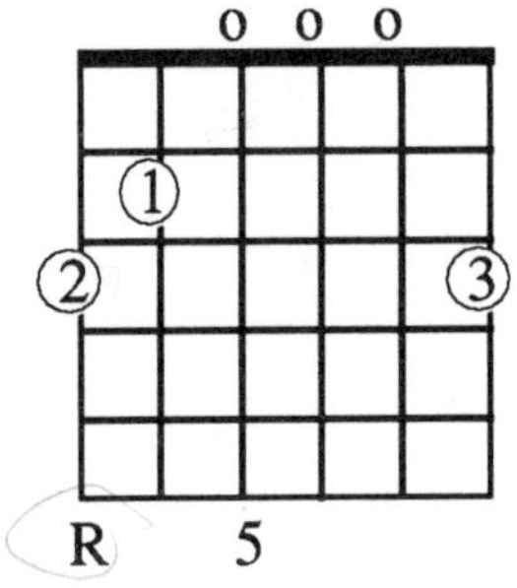

R 5

A7 (V7)

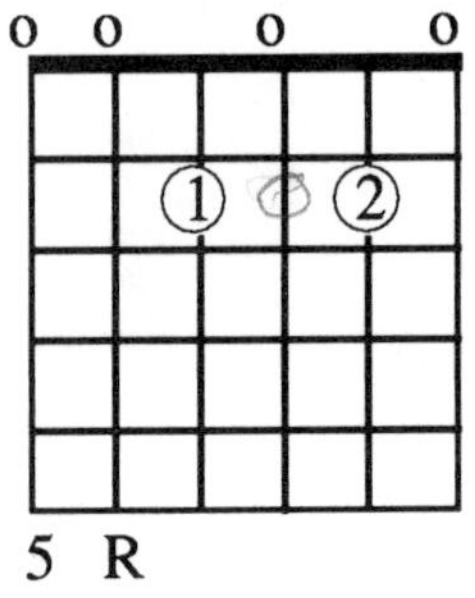

5 R

A

A (I)

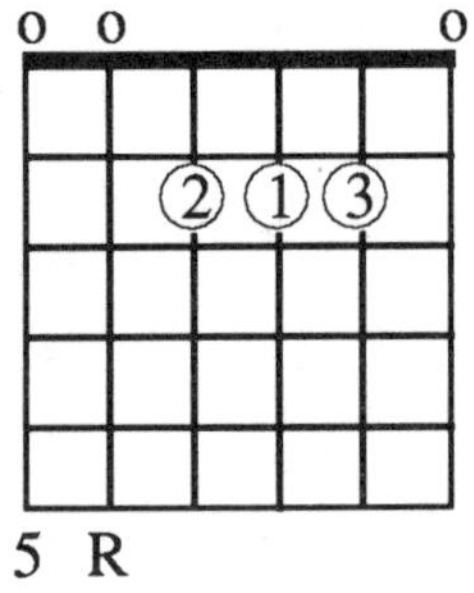

5 R

D (IV)

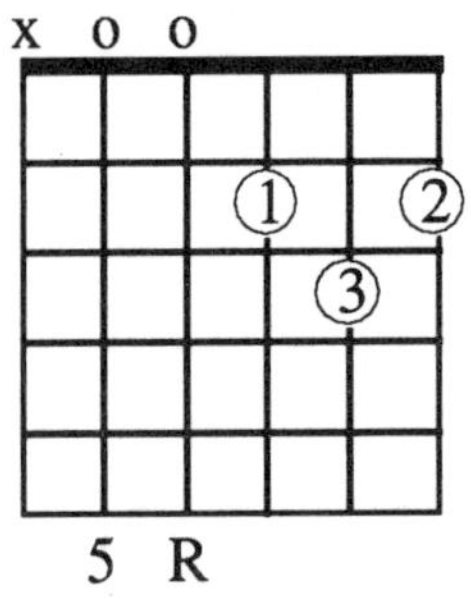

5 R

E7 (V7)

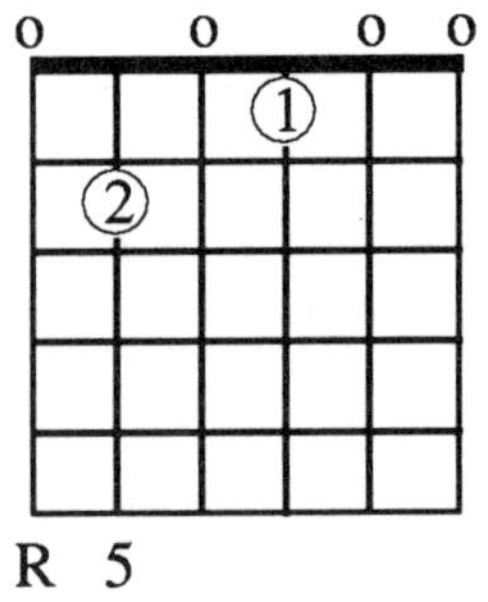

R 5

G

G (I)

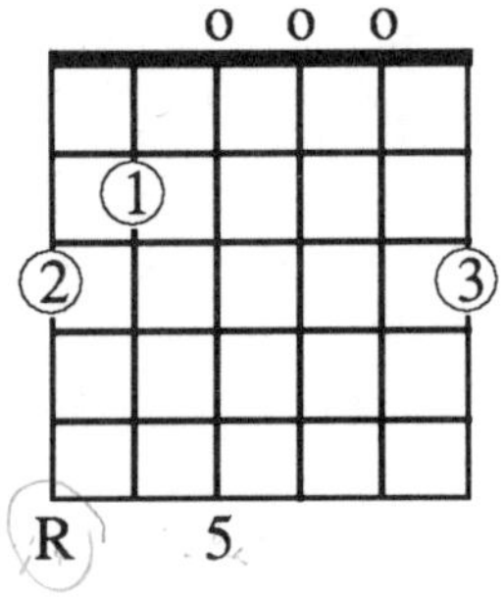

R 5

C (IV)

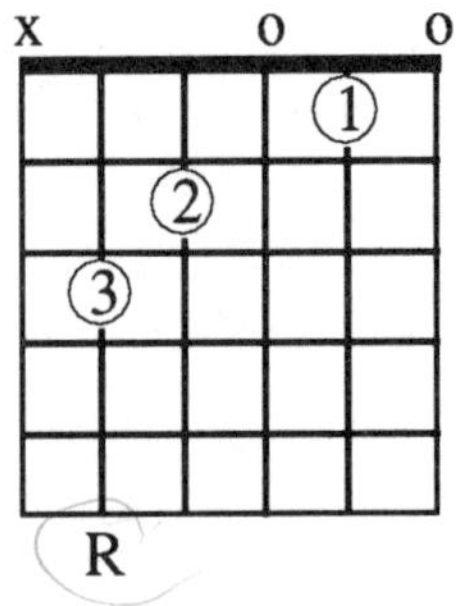

R

D7 (V7)

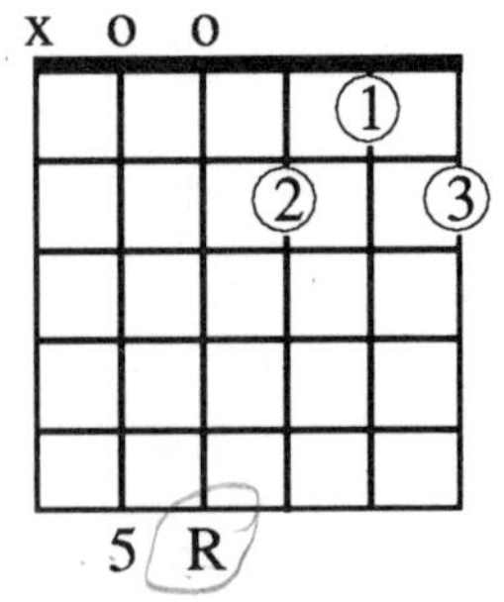

5 R

E

E (I)

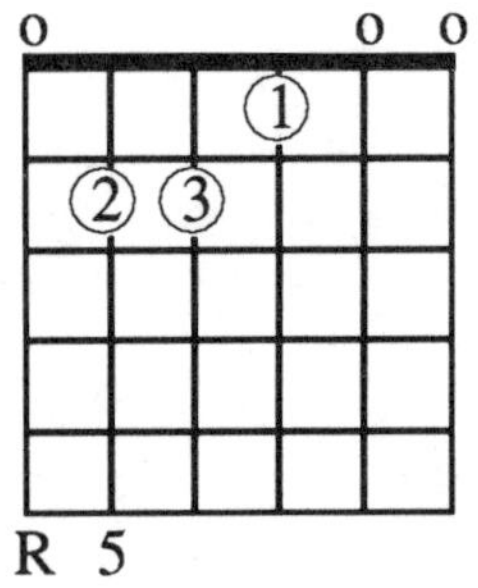

R 5

A (IV)

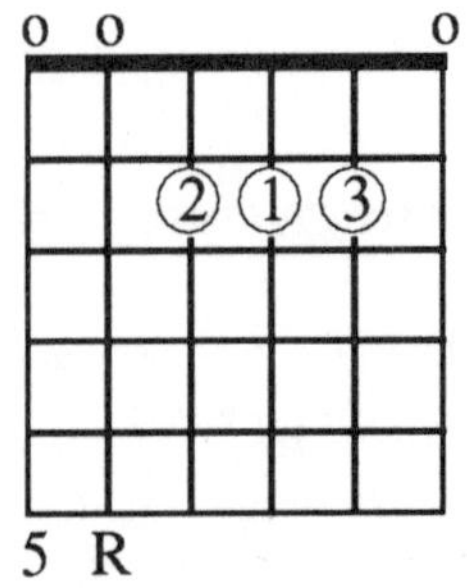

5 R

B7 (V7)

R

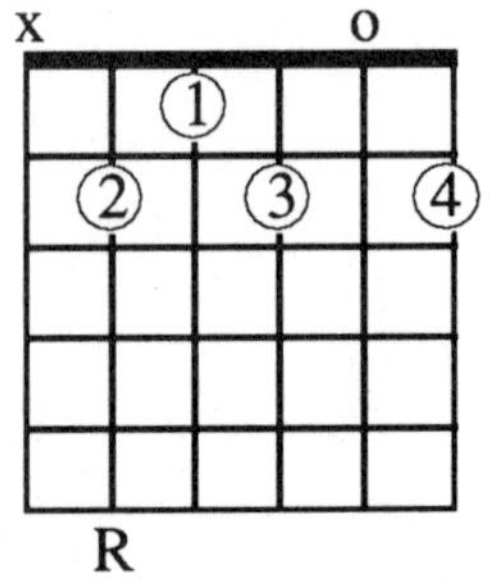

REFERENCE PAGES FOR CHORD PROGRESSIONS IN UNIT ONE

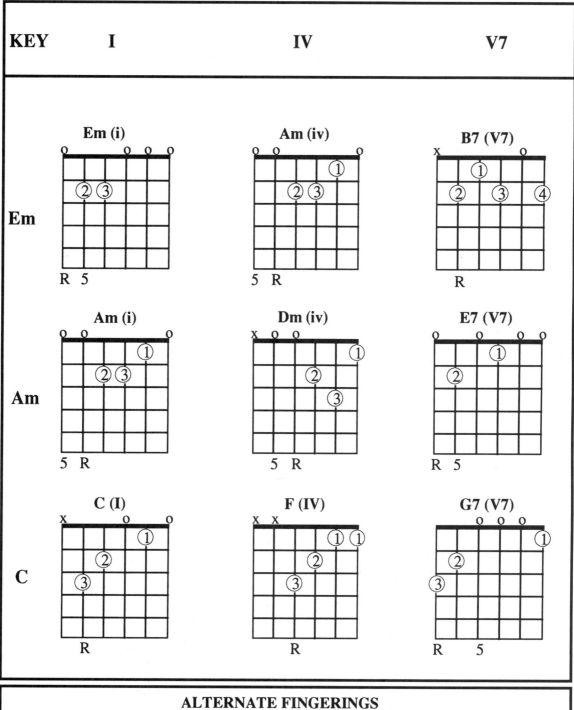

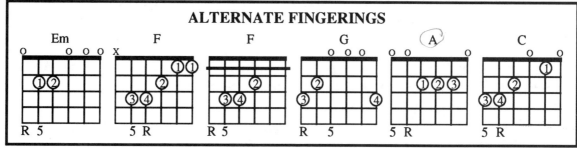

UNIT TWO

PLAYING THE MELODY

Learning to read and play melodies from a printed page of music requires a combination of PHYSICAL and MENTAL skills. To speed progress, you will master these skills SEPARATELY now, combining them later. IT IS VITAL THAT YOU FOLLOW THE UNIT LESSONS IN AN EXACT MANNER. DO THE PHYSICAL SKILL FIRST.

PHYSICAL SKILL: Play a FIRST POSITION SCALE

The word "**position**" when attached to a number, TELLS YOU WHERE ON THE FRETBOARD TO PLACE THE FIRST FINGER OF YOUR LEFT HAND. **FIRST POSITION** means that the first finger of the left hand is to be placed in the first fret, the second finger in the second fret, the third in the third fret and the fourth in the fourth fret. (The same relative fingering applies in other positions. For example, in second position finger 1 will play in fret 2, finger 2 in fret 3, finger 3 in fret 4 and finger 4 in fret 5.) Chart A below shows finger placement for a scale in FIRST POSITION. Chart B replaces these numbers with the letter name for each note.

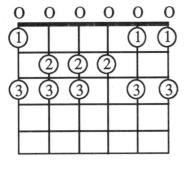 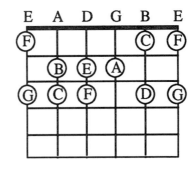

CHART A   CHART B

LEARN THIS FIRST POSITION SCALE, USING THE METHOD BELOW.

1) Using the right thumb, play the three notes on string 6, one note at a time. Play the open position, then 1st fret, then 3rd fret (Chart A). BE SURE TO USE FINGER 1 FOR FRET 1 AND FINGER 3 FOR FRET 3. Do this until your fingers automatically go to the correct frets. KEEP A GOOD POSITION FOR BOTH HANDS.

2) Now, play the 6th string notes as you say the letter names ALOUD (see chart B). This may make you feel silly, but it speeds memorization of the note names. **PLAY AND SAY: E - F - G**. Then play and say it backward: **G - F - E**.

3) When you can do this without looking at your left hand, go on to the 5th string notes. Follow steps 1 and 2 in learning string 5.

4) Now, put strings 6 and 5 together, playing and saying: **E - F - G - A - B - C.** Then, do it backward: **C - B - A - G - F - E.**

5) Following this procedure, continue until the notes of all six strings are learned. Be sure you can PLAY AND SAY the entire scale, going both directions, without looking at the charts. **FINGERINGS AND HAND POSITIONS MUST BE PERFECT.** To avoid boredom, alternate physical practice with mastery of the following.

MENTAL SKILL: READING NOTATION

NOTES, when placed on the staff, tell the musician which pitch (tone) to play. The **NOTE HEAD** (see p. 24) may be placed on any line or space within, above or below the five-line staff. The **placement** of the note head tells you which pitch to play.

The music alphabet contains 7 letters: A, B, C, D, E, F, G. These letters, when applied to sequential notation, appear CONSECUTIVELY on the staff as line-space-line-space.

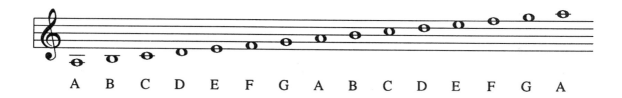

Each line or space represents a specific pitch. Using the key below, **MEMORIZE THE LINE NOTES OF THE TREBLE CLEF.**

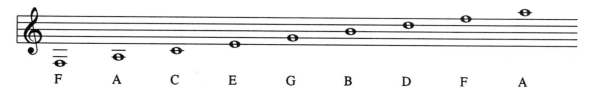

MEMORIZE THE SPACE NOTES OF THE TREBLE CLEF.

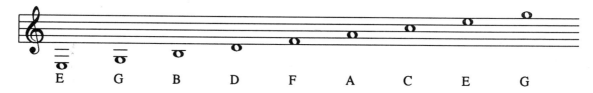

DO WORK SHEET 1, p. 109. Refer to this page only when necessary.

COUNTING

NOTES AND RESTS

You know that the placement of the NOTE HEAD tells you which pitch to play. **The KIND OF NOTE attached to the head tells you HOW LONG to hold each pitch.**

THE PARTS OF THE NOTE ARE: HEAD, STEM, FLAG (or BEAM)

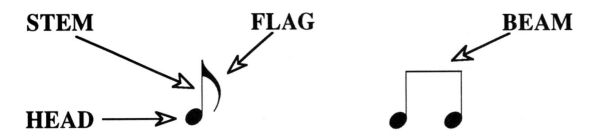

MEMORIZE THE KINDS OF NOTES BELOW.

o   **WHOLE**

♩   **HALF**

♩   **QUARTER**

♫ ♪ **EIGHTH** (a single 8th note has a flag; two or more may be written with a connecting beam)

The chart below left graphically illustrates the relative value of the kinds of notes above. The note addition table below right is another way of looking at note relationships.

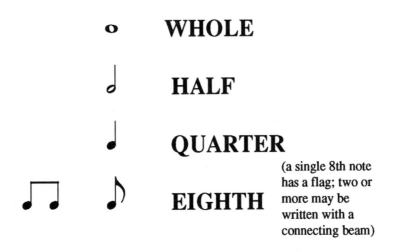

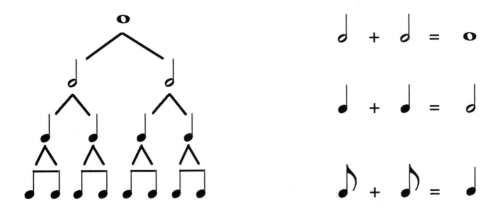

SILENCE is an important element of music. For each kind of note, there is a corresponding **REST** representing silence. **MEMORIZE THE RESTS.**

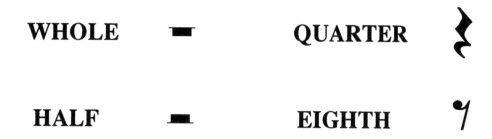

WHOLE ▬	**QUARTER**
HALF ▬	**EIGHTH**

Study the illustrations below.

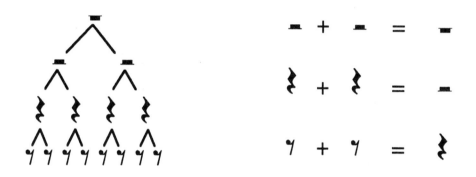

FIND THE ANSWERS TO THE NOTE AND REST ADDITION BELOW.
Each correct answer is a SINGLE SYMBOL.

♩ + ♩ =	♪ + ♩ + ♪ + ♩ =	𝄽 + 𝄽 =		
♩ + ♩ =	♩ + ♫ =	+ =		
♪ + ♪ =	♫♫ + ♩ =	▬ + ▬ =		
♩ + ♪ + ♪ =	♫♫ =	▬ + 𝄽 + + =		
♩ + ♩ + ♩ =	♩ + ♩ + ♫ =	+ + 𝄽 =		

THE TIME SIGNATURE

At this point, you need to understand the entire time signature. You already know that **THE TOP NUMBER TELLS YOU THE NUMBER OF BEATS IN A MEASURE.**

THE BOTTOM NUMBER REPRESENTS THE KIND OF NOTE RECEIVING ONE BEAT.

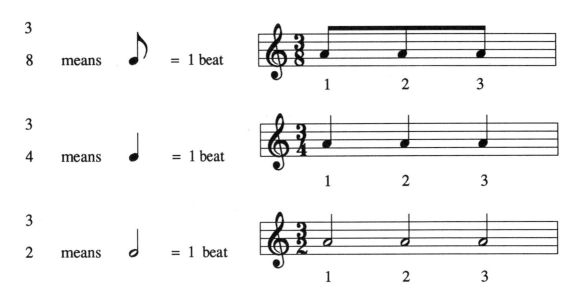

Sometimes you will find both notes and rests in a measure. Here are some examples, with the beats shown below the notation.

HOW TO COUNT WHEN ♩ = 1 BEAT

Your first songs will contain a "4" as the bottom number of the time signature. Therefore the notes and rests will receive the following beats:

♪	or	𝄾	=	1/2 beat
♩	or	𝄽	=	1 beat
𝅗𝅥	or	𝄼	=	2 beats
𝅝	or	𝄻	=	4 beats

In order to correctly count the music you play, it helps to write in the counting below the notes and rests. This is easy to do. Follow the examples below.

EACH HALF-BEAT IS REPRESENTED BY ONE WRITTEN SYMBOL (either a number or "+"). THEREFORE, IN ONE MEASURE OF 4/4 TIME, YOU WILL ALWAYS WRITE: 1 + 2 + 3 + 4 +.

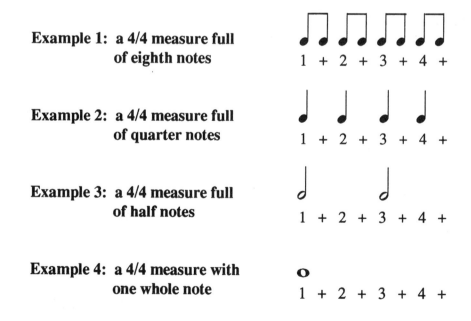

Example 1: a 4/4 measure full of eighth notes

♫ ♫ ♫ ♫
1 + 2 + 3 + 4 +

Example 2: a 4/4 measure full of quarter notes

♩ ♩ ♩ ♩
1 + 2 + 3 + 4 +

Example 3: a 4/4 measure full of half notes

𝅗𝅥 𝅗𝅥
1 + 2 + 3 + 4 +

Example 4: a 4/4 measure with one whole note

𝅝
1 + 2 + 3 + 4 +

PLAY THESE MEASURES USING ANY PITCH. COUNT OUT LOUD AS YOU PLAY.

DO WORK SHEET 2, p. 110.

TIES AND DOTS

A **TIE** connects **TWO NOTES OF IDENTICAL PITCH.** It tells you to play the first note
and then HOLD it for the additional value of the second note. **COUNT AND PLAY THE
LINES BELOW.** It helps to write in the counting.

A DOT FOLLOWING A NOTE ADDS HALF THE NOTE'S VALUE.

IF ♩ = 1 beat, then ♩. = 1 + 1/2 = 1 1/2 beats

IF ♩ = 2 beats, then ♩. = 2 + 1 = 3 beats

IF 𝅝 = 4 beats, then 𝅝. = 4 + 2 = 6 beats

WRITE IN THE COUNTING. PLAY WHILE COUNTING OUT LOUD.

RHYTHM LINES FOR PRACTICE AND REFERENCE

COUNT OUT LOUD EVENLY AND PLAY WITH YOUR COUNTING.

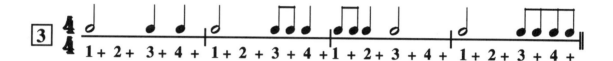

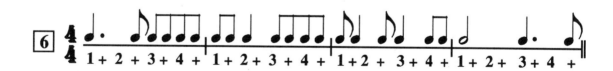

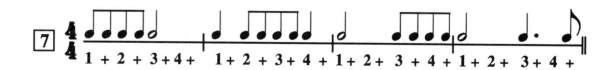

30

RHYTHM LINES FOR PRACTICE AND REFERENCE

COUNT OUT LOUD EVENLY AND PLAY WITH YOUR COUNTING.

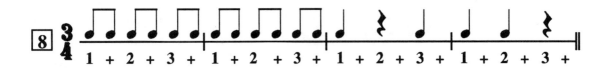

COMBINE THE PHYSICAL AND MENTAL SKILLS:
NOTATION OF THE FIRST POSITION SCALE

Now you can connect the first position scale to the notation representing it. Below are your fingering and note name charts. Beneath them are two lines of notation showing how this scale looks when written in WHOLE notes.

PLAY THE SCALE AS YOU WATCH THE NOTES. SAY THE LETTER NAMES AS YOU GO. AVOID LOOKING AT YOUR LEFT HAND. THE IDEA HERE IS TO CONNECT THE WRITTEN SYMBOL TO THE MUSCLE PATTERNS YOU HAVE SO CAREFULLY DEVELOPED.

Don't forget that the music alphabet repeats itself. For instance, there are three G's in this scale. Each has a **SPECIFIC SOUND** and is **NOTATED IN A SPECIFIC PLACE ON THE STAFF**. Don't get them confused.

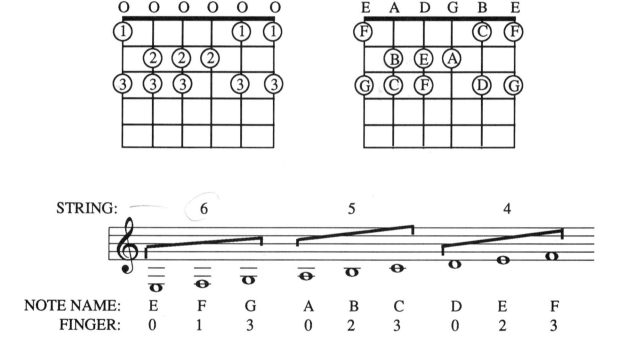

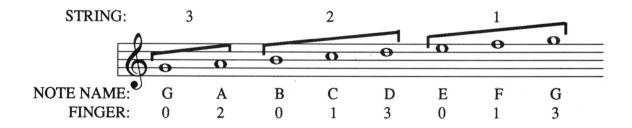

DO WORK SHEET 3, p. 111.

32

FINALLY, YOU'RE READY TO PLAY MELODIES.
These melodies are arranged so that you learn the notes on just two strings at a time. You will begin with strings 6 and 5 and go up from there. Follow the instructions below.

1. **USE FIRST POSITION FINGERINGS .**
2. **WRITE IN THE COUNTING BELOW THE NOTATION.**
3. **DO NOT WRITE IN THE NAMES OF THE LETTERS!!!!!!!**

MELODIES USING NOTES ON STRINGS 6 AND 5 ONLY

WHEN YOU CAN PLAY THESE MELODIES ACCURATELY AND SMOOTHLY, GO TO THE NEXT PAGE.

MELODIES USING NOTES ON STRINGS 4 AND 3 (plus)

DON'T FORGET TO WRITE IN YOUR COUNTING.

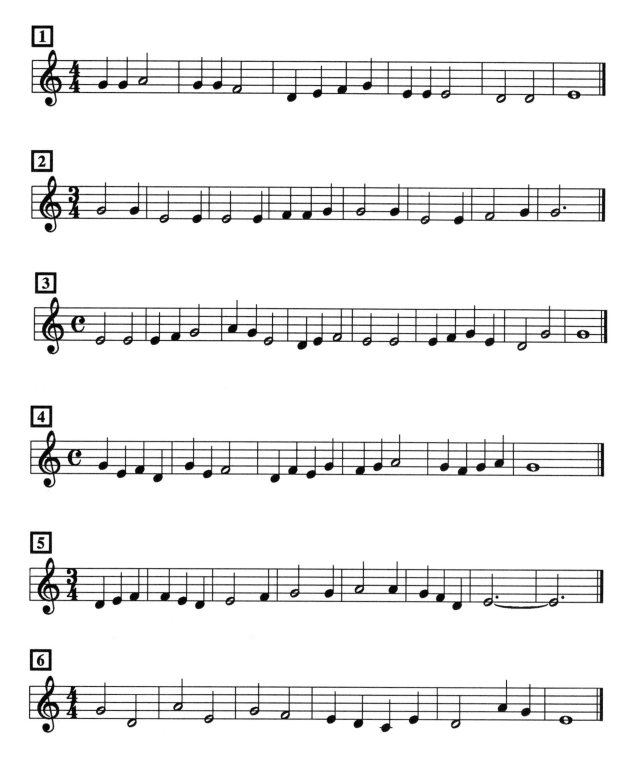

WHEN YOU CAN PLAY THIS PAGE ACCURATELY, GO TO THE NEXT PAGE.

MELODIES USING NOTES ON STRINGS 2 AND 1 (plus some)

A gentle reminder: COUNT OUT LOUD
KEEP A GOOD POSITION IN BOTH HANDS

PLAYING TRIOS

When you have completed this page, you will be able to join with two other guitarists to play the trios which follow. Each trio is made up of 3 lines of music to be played AT THE SAME TIME. Player I takes line 1, player II takes line 2 and player III, line 3. Players should COUNT TOGETHER for two full measures before beginning to play together.

TRIOS, USING MELODIC LINES YOU ALREADY KNOW

SHARPS, FLATS, NATURALS, ENHARMONIC NOTES

Chart A below is the one you know well. You probably noticed that there were some frets you didn't play when we did this first position scale. Chart A shows **NATURAL NOTES**. Chart B shows the pitches which occur in the frets between the natural notes. (Use finger 4 to play notes at the 4th fret.)

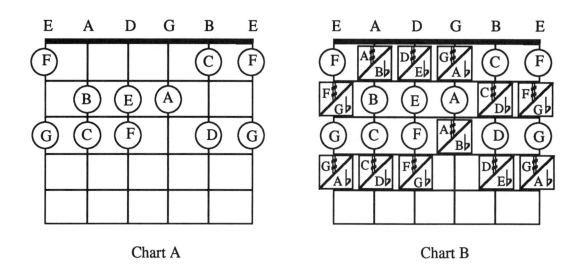

Chart A   Chart B

MEMORIZE THE SYMBOLS AND DEFINITIONS BELOW.

A SHARP (♯) RAISES A NATURAL NOTE ONE FRET. Fret 2 on the first string is, therefore, F♯.

Notation: Played: ② F♯

A FLAT (♭) LOWERS A NATURAL NOTE ONE FRET. Fret 2 on the first string is, therefore, also called G♭.

Notation: Played: ② G♭

F♯ and G♭ are called **ENHARMONIC NOTES.**

ENHARMONIC means: SAME SOUND, DIFFERENT NAMES.

38

A SHARP OR FLAT INSERTED IN A MEASURE LASTS FOR THE AFFECTED NOTE FOR THAT ENTIRE MEASURE. IT IS CANCELLED BY THE BAR LINE AT THE END OF THE MEASURE. In the example below, all the G's in measure 1 will be sharped. However, the G in measure 2 will be a natural G since the sharp was cancelled by the intervening bar line. The **NATURAL (♮)** is used to cancel a sharp or flat. It simply means: play the natural note. Measure 3 below contains a natural. (The natural in parentheses, measure 2, is a "courtesy natural". It reminds the player of the intervening bar line.)

You know that an Arabic number (1, 2, 3) indicates left hand finger use. An Arabic number inside a circle (①, ②, ③) indicates the STRING on which a note is found. The B♭ in measure 4 below is to be played on string 3 (③) with finger 3. **PLAY THE TUNE WHICH FOLLOWS.**

The entire fretboard of the guitar is made up of **HALF-STEPS.** From any one fret to the next, going up or down, is a half-step. If you were to play a series of 12 half-steps in order, it would be called a **CHROMATIC SCALE.**

LEARN TO PLAY THE TWO SCALES BELOW. Notice that the flat or sharp is written DIRECTLY IN FRONT OF THE NOTE AFFECTED. Just as the line or space of the staff passes directly through the note head, the same line or space goes directly through the middle of the sharp or flat head.

THE CHROMATIC SCALE, ASCENDING AND DESCENDING

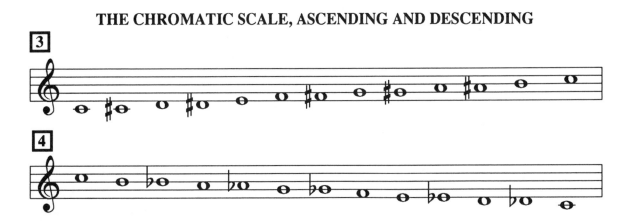

DO WORK SHEET 4, p. 112.

THE KEY SIGNATURE

At the beginning of each piece of music, between the treble clef and the time signature, you will find the KEY SIGNATURE.

IF THERE IS NOTHING BETWEEN THE TREBLE CLEF AND THE TIME SIGNATURE, IT MEANS THAT THERE ARE NO SHARPS OR FLATS PLAYED IN THE SONG, EXCEPT WHERE SPECIFICALLY WRITTEN IN (example 1).

HOWEVER, IF THERE ARE SHARPS OR FLATS THERE, IT MEANS THAT THE AFFECTED NOTES ARE TO BE SHARPED OR FLATTED THROUGHOUT THE ENTIRE SONG (examples 2-6).

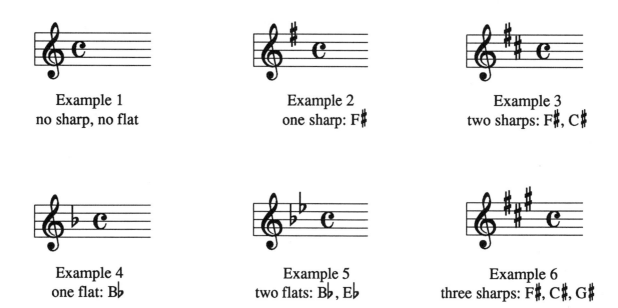

Example 1
no sharp, no flat

Example 2
one sharp: F♯

Example 3
two sharps: F♯, C♯

Example 4
one flat: B♭

Example 5
two flats: B♭, E♭

Example 6
three sharps: F♯, C♯, G♯

Below is an example of music with a key signature (one sharp, F♯) appearing between the treble clef and the time signature. This key signature tells you that all F's in the piece are to be sharped.

A MORE COMPLETE EXPLANATION OF KEY SIGNATURES WILL FOLLOW IN A LATER SECTION OF THIS BOOK. FOR NOW, JUST BE SURE YOU ARE SHARPING OR FLATTING THE CORRECT PITCHES IF YOU PLAY A SONG WITH FLATS OR SHARPS IN THE KEY SIGNATURE.

40

FIRST POSITION TUNES

Write in the counting before you play (we've helped out with the last tune).

University Fight Song

Scott Joplin

4   +   1 + 2 +   3 + 4 +   1+2+3 + 4   +   1 +   2 + 3 + 4 +

ADDITIONAL FIRST POSITION EXERCISES

You may use these exercises for additional first position practice, as an introduction to sight-reading or in preparation for exams. In any case, attempt to keep your eyes on the music without sneaking peeks at your left hand. Watch out for key signatures.

UNIT THREE

PLAYING BASS

You know how to play two of the elements needed for a three-player combo: rhythm and melody. All you need now is a simple bass line, which you can learn on your acoustic guitar.

THE FOUR STRINGS OF THE ELECTRIC BASS ARE THE SAME AS STRINGS 3, 4, 5 AND 6 ON YOUR ACOUSTIC GUITAR.

To play a basic bass line, you will use the root and fifth for each rhythm chord designated in the music. HOWEVER, YOU WILL FIND THE ROOT (R) AND FIFTH (5) IN A DIFFERENT WAY THAN YOU DID IN UNIT ONE.

The root and fifth for all natural note chords are shown on the next page. Find the diagram for G. Place fingers 1 and 3. **NOTICE THAT THE FIFTH IS FOUND ON THE STRING NEXT HIGHEST FROM THE ROOT STRING AND TWO FRETS HIGHER.** This relationship is the SAME FOR ALL CHORDS. If you always place your first finger on the root, the fifth is ALWAYS ON THE NEXT HIGHEST STRING, TWO FRETS HIGHER, easily playable with finger 3. Learn the root and fifth positions for the G and C chords (next page).

PLAY THE SAMPLE LINE BELOW, WITH ONE PERSON ON RHYTHM AND ONE ON BASS. While the rhythm player strums the G chord, the bass player plays the root and fifth for G on beats 1 and 3 of each measure. When the rhythm moves to the C chord, the bass player plays the root and fifth for C.

```
RHYTHM:        G / / / | / / / / | C / / / | / / / /‖
BASS:          R    5  | R    5  | R    5  | R    5 ‖
          4
BEATS:    4    1 2 3 4 | 1 2 3 4 | 1 2 3 4 | 1 2 3 4‖
```

FINALLY, to get good, clear bass notes you will want to play the A and D bass parts on the frets shown in the diagrams which follow. These are the root note positions you used when tuning the guitar. They give you a better control of the bass part. You may play the bass parts for E chords in either of the two places shown, depending on the sound you like.

+---+
| **IMPORTANT** |
| |
| **THE ROOT IS THE SAME FOR ALL CHORDS BASED ON** |
| **A SINGLE NOTE. FOR INSTANCE, "D" IS THE ROOT OF** |
| **ALL THESE CHORDS: D, Dm, Dm7, D7.** |
+---+

ROOT/FIFTH BASS PART DIAGRAMS FOR NATURAL NOTES

A	B	C	D
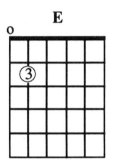	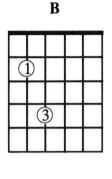	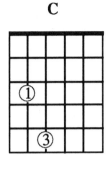	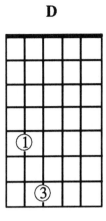

E	E	F	G
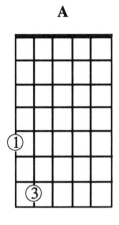	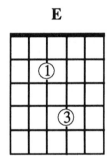	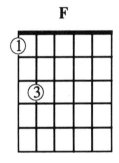	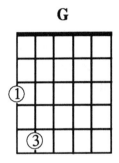

SAMPLE BASS/RHYTHM CHARTS

> NOTE: ⅔ means to repeat the previous measure

1

```
Rhythm: 4  D / / /    ⅔  A7 / / /    ⅔  D / / /  A7 / / /  D ‖
Bass:   4  R    5         R    5        R    5    R    5    R
```

2

```
4  D / / /   ⅔  G / / /   ⅔  A7 / / /   ⅔  D / / /  A7 / / /  D ‖
4  R    5       R   5        R    5         R    5   R    5    R
```

3

```
4  G / / /  Em / / /  Am / / /  D / / /  G / / /  D / / /  G ‖
4  R    5   R    5    R    5    R   5    R   5    R   5    R
```

4

```
3  C / / / / / /  E7 / / / / / /  A7 / / / / / /  D7 / / / / / /  G7 / / / / / /  C ‖
4  R      5       R      5        R      5        R      5        R      5        R
```

PLAYING THE THREE-PERSON COMBO

You may now put together your own combos, using tunes you like. One example is shown here. With two of your friends, play "Aura Lee" from the music below. One person plays the melody, another strums rhythm and the third plays bass.

In this example, for the first time, you will have measure numbers at the beginning of each line. These are often helpful in ensemble play. Use them as you rehearse.

AURA LEE

Chords often change in the middle of a measure, as in measure ll of Aura Lee. In this case, you should play the root of the new chord WHEN IT APPEARS, regardless of the beat on which this occurs.

WHEN YOU HAVE FINISHED THIS SONG you may form a trio, following the instructions of your teacher. Choose your own music for performance from the back of this book or from supplementary materials. SELECT AN EASY MELODY. If that melody is in 3/4 time, be sure to review the previous page for an example of application of R and 5 in the bass line.

UNIT FOUR

PLAYING BARRE CHORDS

Full (grand) barre chords are MOVABLE chords in which the first finger is placed across all strings in a given fret

(this is the BARRE) and other fingers are placed in a position below the barre. The picture at left shows a barre chord; the first finger has placed a barre across all strings in fret l and the E chord has been formed below the barre, using fingers 2, 3 and 4. The picture at right illustrates proper thumb placement when playing a barre chord.

To understand the formation of barre chords, it is essential to know:

1) HOW AND WHERE TO PLACE THE FINGERS BELOW THE BARRE and

2) HOW AND WHERE TO PLACE THE BARRE

FORMING BARRE CHORDS USING E, E7, Em and Em7

STEP 1: **LEARN NEW FINGERINGS** for the chords below. Notice that you will not use finger l in these new diagrams. That is because you use this finger to form the barre. **AS YOU LEARN THESE NEW FINGERINGS, SAY THE NAME OF EACH CHORD AS YOU PLAY.** This will help to ensure that you don't confuse the different types of E chords. Practice these until the finger patterns become automatic.

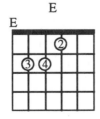

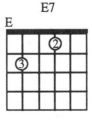

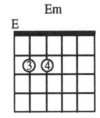

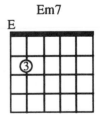

STEP 2: LEARN WHERE TO PLACE THE BARRE. You know that from one fret to the next (going up or down) is called a half-step. Two half-steps equal one whole step. Therefore, if you move two frets on the guitar, you move one whole step.

MEMORIZE THE HALF AND WHOLE STEPS ON THE "E" STRING, AS SHOWN BELOW RIGHT. Note that the half-steps occur at only two places: B - C and E - F. All other distances are whole steps.

To correctly play the barre, place finger 1 COMPLETELY across all strings with the fingertip slightly over the edge of the fretboard (see picture on previous page). ROTATE the elbow about two inches **IN TOWARD THE BODY so that both the bone and the flesh** of the finger are touching the strings. This makes it easier to press down.

DO THE FOLLOWING EXERCISE TO SPEED MEMORIZATION.

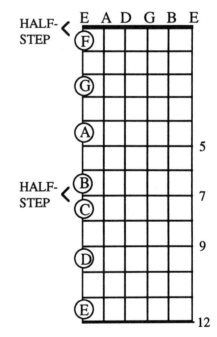

1) Play the low E (string 6) open.

2) Place your left hand finger 1 across the first fret in barre position (see picture on previous page). WITH THE RIGHT THUMB, PLAY THE SINGLE NOTE "F" ON STRING 6. SAY THE NOTE NAME AS YOU PLAY.

3) Move left hand finger 1 to the THIRD fret in barre position. PLAY THE SINGLE NOTE "G" ON STRING 6. SAY "G" AS YOU PLAY.

4) Following the procedure used in steps 2 and 3, play all natural notes on string 6.

   PLAY AND SAY: E - F - G - A - B - C - D - E

5) Now do it backward.

   PLAY AND SAY: E - D - C - B - A - G - F - E

6) Practice until you can do this exercise without looking at the chart.

7) Just to be sure you remember the application of sharps and flats to natural notes, go up the "E" string by half-steps, saying all the note names (E - F - F♯ - G, etc.) until you reach the 12th fret. Then come back down the string, saying the enharmonic flat names (E - E♭ - D - D♭ - C - B, etc.).

You have now mastered the two elements needed to form movable barre chords using the E type chords.

1) new fingerings for the the E types,

2) names of the pitches on the E string.

We will now combine these two elements to form new chords. Place your left hand in the positions shown in the diagrams below. **DO NOT STRUM. SIMPLY WORK ON LEFT HAND PLACEMENT. PAY CLOSE ATTENTION TO CORRECT POSITIONING OF THE LEFT THUMB.** Refer to the pictures at the beginning of the unit if necessary.

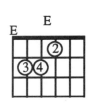

1) This is the E chord. The ROOT, E, is on string 6.

2) This is the F chord. The barre is placed on fret 1 with the E chord below it. All strings which were open in the E diagram have been moved ONE HALF-STEP HIGHER BY PLACING THE BARRE. The chord form has also been moved up one half-step. THE NEW CHORD, THEREFORE, IS F, ONE HALF-STEP ABOVE THE E CHORD. The ROOT, F, is on string 6. (The letters placed on the barre in these diagrams are for learning purposes only. They will not appear in a standard chord chart.)

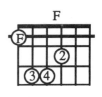

3) This form looks just like the F chord, except it is two frets (one whole step) higher. ONE WHOLE STEP ABOVE F IS G. Therefore, this is the G chord. The root is found on string 6.

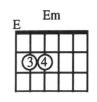

4) This is the Em chord. The root is on string 6.

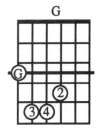

5) This is the Fm chord, which you will form in the same way you formed F. The barre moves the open strings one half-step and the Em chord form moves one half-step. The root is on string 6.

6) This is the Gm chord, formed exactly as you did the Fm chord, except that it is one whole step higher. The root is on string 6.

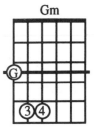

7) This is E7. The root of the chord is on string 6.

10) This is Em7.

8) This is F7, moved in the same way you moved previously.

11) This is Fm7, one half-step above Em7.

9) This is G7, one whole step higher than the F7 chord.

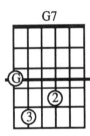

12) This is Gm7, one whole step above Fm7.

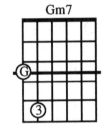

IMPORTANT NOTE:
IF YOU MOVE ANY "E" TYPE (E, Em, E7, Em7)
UNDER THE BARRE, THE ROOT WILL ALWAYS
BE FOUND ON STRING 6.

PLAY THE EXERCISES ON THE NEXT PAGE, SAYING THE NAME OF EACH CHORD AS YOU PLAY. KEEP ALL FINGERS IN CONTACT WITH THE STRINGS AS YOU MOVE FROM CHORD TO CHORD.

Caution: You may be distressed at the sound you get when you play barre chords. Be patient. You will gradually develop the strength to get a good sound. In the meantime, **BE SURE TO KEEP A GOOD LEFT HAND POSITION AND A POSITIVE ATTITUDE.** If your left hand tires or becomes cramped during practice, rest it. You may also do these drills WITHOUT PUTTING PRESSURE ON THE BARRE CHORD AND WITHOUT STRUMMING WITH THE RIGHT HAND. Just work on correct placement of the chords. This takes the stress from the left hand and still gives you practice in forming the chords properly.

PLAY THESE EXERCISES USING MOVABLE "E" BARRE CHORDS.
STRUM 4 TIMES FOR EACH CHORD.

1) E - F - G - A - B - C - D

2) Em - Fm - Gm - Am - Bm - Cm - Dm

3) E7 - F7 - G7 - A7 - B7 - C7 - D7

4) Em7 - Fm7 - Gm7 - Am7 - Bm7 - Cm7 - Dm7

5) Do the above exercises backward. **SAY THE CHORD NAMES AS YOU PLAY.**

6) Now, move the barre chords BY HALF STEPS. SAY THE SHARP NAMES AS YOU
GO UP AND THE FLAT NAMES AS YOU COME DOWN.
REMEMBER: **ENHARMONIC MEANS SAME SOUND, DIFFERENT NAME.**

E - F - F♯- G - G♯- A - A♯- B - C - C♯- D

D - D♭ - C - B - B♭ - A - A♭- G - G♭- F - E

7) Practice the movable minor, minor seventh and seventh chords, using all frets as you did
in exercises 6 and 7. SAY THE SHARP PITCHES ASCENDING and the FLAT
PITCHES DESCENDING.

DO WORK SHEET 5, p. 113.

APPLYING MOVABLE "E" BARRE CHORDS TO PROGRESSIONS

It is possible to play any song using barre chords. Practice the progressions below, using
movable E types.

1) G - C - D7 - G	3) C - Am - Dm - G7 - C
2) F - B♭- C7 - F	4) F♯m - Bm - C♯7 - F♯m

Now, try playing some of the songs at the back of the book, using only barre chords. Start
with "Amazing Grace", page 102.

FORMING BARRE CHORDS USING THE MOVABLE "A" CHORDS

Now that you understand how to move the E types beneath the barre, it will be very simple to move the A types. We will follow exactly the same procedure.

STEP 1: LEARN THE NEW FINGERINGS FOR THE "A" CHORDS BELOW. MEMORIZE THEM CAREFULLY. (AM7 = A MAJOR 7)

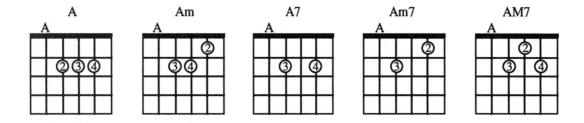

STEP 2: PLACING THE BARRE FOR MOVABLE "A" TYPES

1) Play the A string open. SAY "A".

2) Place the barre on fret 2. Play B, the note ON STRING 5. SAY THE NOTE NAME AS YOU PLAY.

3) Place the barre on fret 3. Play C, the note ON STRING 5. SAY "C".

4) Following the procedure used in steps 2 and 3, play all natural notes on string 5.

   PLAY AND SAY: A - B - C - D - E - F - G

   BACKWARD: A - G - F - E - D - C - B - A

5) Practice until you can do this exercise without looking at the chart.

6) Now move the barre by half-steps. Say the sharp names ascending and the flat names descending.

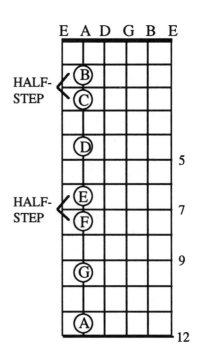

Now that you have mastered the two basic elements for moving the "A" positions, combine them to form new chords. Follow carefully the diagrams on the next page. **DO NOT STRUM. CONCENTRATE ON YOUR LEFT HAND POSITION.**

> # IMPORTANT ITEM!!!!
> ## WHEN YOU MOVE AN "A" TYPE (A, Am, A7, Am7, AM7) THE ROOT OF THE NEW CHORD IS ALWAYS FOUND UNDER THE BARRE ON STRING 5.

1) This is the A chord. THE ROOT IS ON STRING 5.

2) This is the B chord. It is one whole step above the A chord. The root is on string 5. We've placed a "B" on the barre at string 5 so you can visualize this. This letter does not appear in a standard chord chart.

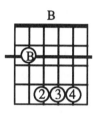

3) This is the C chord. It is one half-step above the B chord. The root is on string 5.

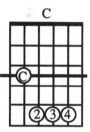

4) The Am chord

7) The A7 chord

5) The Bm chord

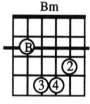

8) The B7 chord

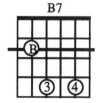

6) The Cm chord

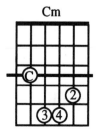

9) The C7 chord

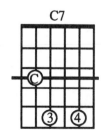

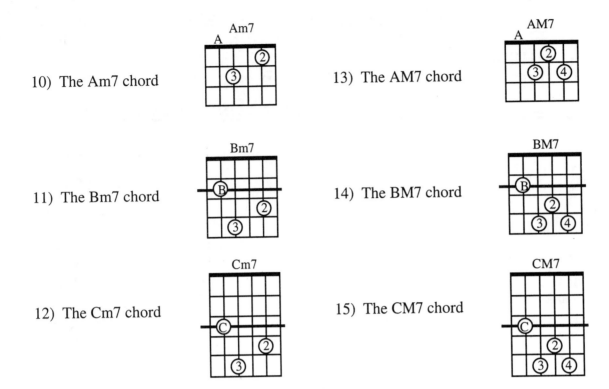

10) The Am7 chord

13) The AM7 chord

11) The Bm7 chord

14) The BM7 chord

12) The Cm7 chord

15) The CM7 chord

USING MOVABLE "A" TYPES, PLAY THE CHORDS BELOW. Follow the same procedures you used in playing the movable "E" types. Play each line forward and backward.

1) A - B - C - D - E - F - G

2) Am - Bm - Cm - Dm - Em - Fm - Gm

3) A7 - B7 - C7 - D7 - E7 - F7 - G7

4) Am7 - Bm7 - Cm7 - Dm7 - Em7 - Fm7 - Gm7

5) AM7 - BM7 - CM7 - DM7 - EM7 - FM7 - GM7

Add the enharmonic chords. Say the sharp names ascending and the flat names descending.

DO WORK SHEET 6, p. 114.

PLAY SOME PROGRESSIONS USING THE "A" TYPE BARRE CHORDS.

1) C - F - G7 - C

2) B - E - F♯7 - B

3) Cm - Fm - G7 - C

4) Bm - Em7 - F♯7 - Bm

5) B♭M7 - E♭ - F7 - B♭M7

6) B♭m7 - C7 - FM7 - B♭m7

Apply the movable "A" types to "Amazing Grace", page 102, and "Rock-a-My Soul", page 101.

COMBINING "E" AND "A" BARRES IN PROGRESSIONS

You have noticed by now that it is awkward to play some of the exercise progressions using only movable E's or A's. This is easily remedied by intermingling the two sets of movable chords so that you don't have to slide the barre so far on some changes. The progressions below can be played by using movable "E" forms for the G chords and movable "A" forms for C and D7.

NOTE THE DIAGRAMS AND PLAY THESE PROGRESSIONS.

1) G - C - D7 - G

2) Gm - Cm - D7 - Gm

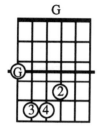
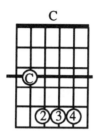
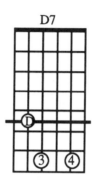
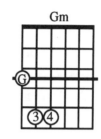
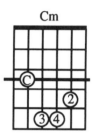

EXPLORING THE BARRE CHORD OPTIONS

> 6 = use a movable "E" form; the ROOT will be on string 6
>
> 5 = use a movable "A" form; the ROOT will be on string 5

Each box below contains two identical progressions, which are to be played using different positions. **Play them with barre chords only,** following the boxed key above.

6 5 6 5 6 1a) F - B♭m - F - C7 - F OR 5 6 5 6 5 1b) F - B♭m - F - C7 - F	6 5 5 6 2a) F - B♭ - C7 - F OR 5 6 6 5 2b) F - B♭ - C7 - F

6   6   5   6 3a) B♭ - Cm - F7 - B♭ OR 5   5   6   5 3b) B♭ - Cm - F7 - B♭

Move now to the music section of the book and play some of the songs using intermingled E and A barre chords. FOR EACH SONG, LOCATE THE EASIEST BARRE POSITIONS FOR PLAY. You may find it helpful to place a "6" or "5" above the chord names.

DO WORK SHEET 7, p. 115.

UNIT FIVE

MAJOR SCALES AND KEY SIGNATURES

The distance from one note to another is an **INTERVAL**. You already know about half-step and whole-step intervals, which you learned in order to play barre chords. You can use that same knowledge now to understand scale construction.

A **SCALE** is an organized series of notes in stepwise order. The most common scale in Western music is the **MAJOR SCALE**. It contains **ONE OCTAVE**, meaning 8 notes.

ANY NOTE MAY BE SELECTED AS THE KEYNOTE. From this keynote, you will simply follow an INTERVAL FORMULA to find the other scale pitches. (If the keynote is not "C", you will have to add sharps or flats to make the formula true.)

> **MEMORIZE THE FORMULA:** | KEYNOTE | **W - W - H - W - W - W - H**
>
> **W = WHOLE STEP   H = HALF-STEP**

THE THREE STEPS USED IN WRITING A MAJOR SCALE ARE ILLUSTRATED BELOW. (We've used "F" as the keynote.)

STEP 1: Draw a treble clef, notate the keynote and the seven following notes.

STEP 2: Enter the major scale formula, as shown below.

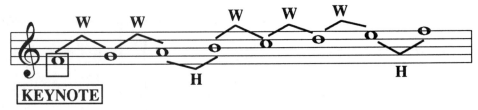

STEP 3: Prove the formula, adding sharps or flats where needed.

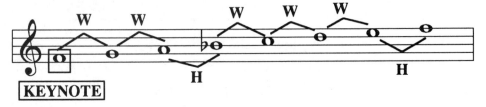

DO WORK SHEET 8, p. 116. WRITE MAJOR SCALES, as directed.

PLAYING MAJOR SCALES IN FIRST POSITION

C MAJOR SCALE

LEARN TO PLAY THIS SCALE IN FIRST POSITION. PROCEED AS FOLLOWS:

1) As you begin, use the right thumb (rest stroke, p. 18) to play the pitches. Keep a perfect and CONSISTENT position for BOTH HANDS. Check them often.

2) **PLAY VERY, VERY, VERY SLOWLY.**

3) When you can play up and down the scale WITHOUT ERROR, move on to a new technique (instructions follow).

PLAYING SCALES WITH ALTERNATING FINGERS

1) **MEMORIZE THE LETTERS USED TO IDENTIFY THE RIGHT HAND FINGERS.** These letters are derived from the Spanish names for the fingers:

> p = pulgar
> i = indicio
> m = medio
> a = anular

2) Place the right hand in the position shown in the picture.

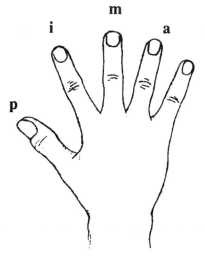

Figure 31

3) Place the "i" finger gently on string 5. PUSH through the string with the "i" finger, playing string 5 and coming to REST on string 6. **THIS IS THE REST STROKE.** (See pictures below.)

Before playing string 5   *After playing string 5*

4) Now, do the same thing with finger "m". Alternate these two fingers so that when one plays, the "resting" finger comes out to its next playing position. When done correctly, this process feels as if your fingers are scissors snapping back and forth.

PLAY.

USING THE PICK TO PLAY SCALES

The flat pick is used in many music styles. You may have used one for strumming in Units One and Four. If not, refer to the pictures at the bottom of page three to review the correct technique for holding the pick.

In this unit, you may apply the pick to the playing of single notes. **IT IS IMPORTANT TO USE BOTH DOWN (⊓) AND UP (∨) STROKES for speed and efficiency.**

NOW PLAY THE PREVIOUS SCALE EXERCISE USING YOUR PICK.

Now, you may apply the alternating "i - m" fingers and the pick to the playing of major scales you need to know.

USE STANDARD FIRST POSITION FINGERING, EXCEPT WHERE NOTED IN THE SECOND OCTAVE OF THE A MAJOR SCALE. OCTAVE = 8 NOTES

C MAJOR, 1 OCTAVE

G MAJOR, 2 OCTAVES

D MAJOR, 1 OCTAVE

A MAJOR, 2 OCTAVES

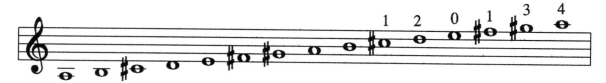

E MAJOR, 2 OCTAVES

F MAJOR, 2 OCTAVES

MORE ABOUT THE KEY SIGNATURE

Most Western composers base their compositions on a scale. Their way of letting the player know which scale they chose for a piece is called the KEY SIGNATURE. (The key signature actually represents two related scales, but for the moment we will only be concerned with one of them.)

You have already seen a key signature. It is found between the treble clef and the time signature at the beginning of a piece.

This is the signature for the C scale, which has no sharps and no flats.

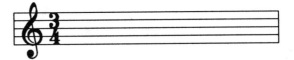

ALL MAJOR SCALES AND THE KEY SIGNATURES WHICH REPRESENT THEM ARE PRINTED HERE. THESE SCALES ARE NOTATED IN ONE-OCTAVE FORM (8 notes).

SCALE   SIGNATURE

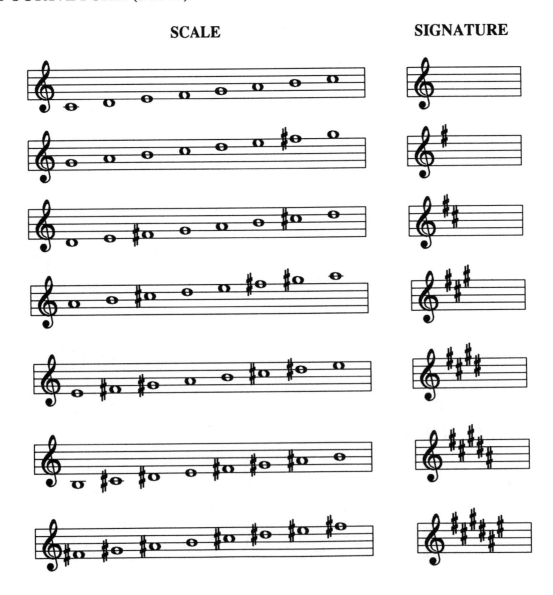

SCALE

SIGNATURE

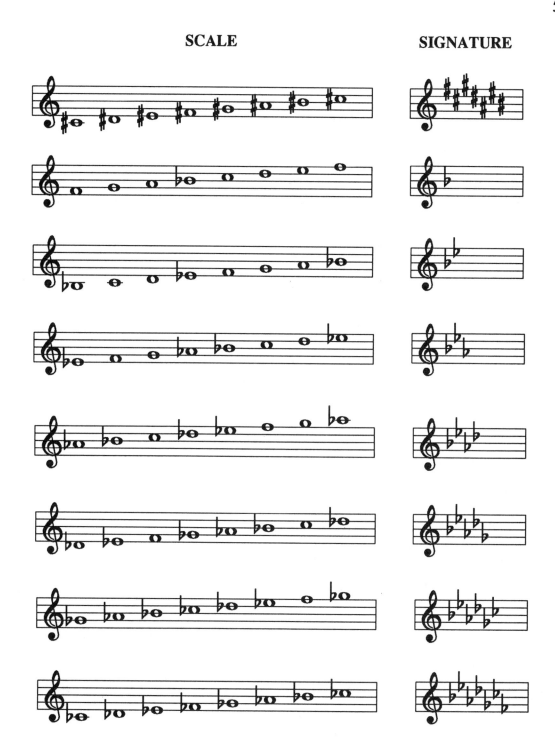

BUT--do you have to memorize all these signatures? NO, just the two shown below.

MEMORIZE THESE:

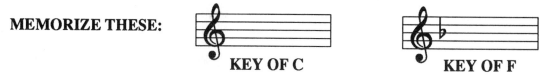

KEY OF C

KEY OF F

For all other signatures, there are simple ways to determine the **KEY** (the scale on which the music is based) by reading the signature.

TO FIND THE KEY IN A *FLAT* SIGNATURE:

1) **LOCATE THE NEXT-TO-LAST FLAT** (read from left to right, just as you are doing for this sentence).

2) **NAME THAT FLAT.** That's the answer.

MEMORIZE THE RULE. Study the examples.

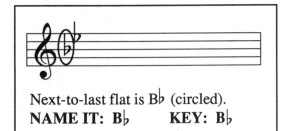

Next-to-last flat is B♭ (circled).
NAME IT: B♭   **KEY: B♭**

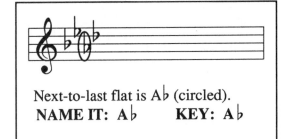

Next-to-last flat is A♭ (circled).
NAME IT: A♭   **KEY: A♭**

TO FIND THE KEY IN A *SHARP* SIGNATURE:

1) **LOCATE THE LAST SHARP. PLAY THAT SHARP ON YOUR GUITAR.**

2) **GO UP 1/2 STEP. THAT'S THE KEY.**

MEMORIZE THE RULE. Study the examples.

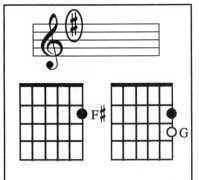

1) LAST SHARP: F♯

2) HALF-STEP UP: G

   KEY: G

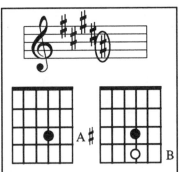

1) LAST SHARP: A♯

2) HALF-STEP UP: B

   KEY: B

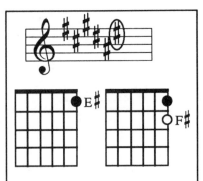

1) LAST SHARP: E♯

2) HALF-STEP UP: F♯

   KEY: F♯

DO WORK SHEET 9, p. 117.

UNIT SIX

DEVELOPMENT OF THE RIGHT HAND: ARPEGGIOS

PLACE THE RIGHT HAND IN CORRECT POSITION. IMITATE THE PICTURES.

Place the right hand on the strings OVER THE SOUND HOLE in the following way:

1) place "i" finger on string 3
2) place "m" finger on string 2
3) place "a" finger on string 1

CORRECT MOVEMENT OF THE THUMB IS CRITICAL TO GOOD PLAYING. IT SHOULD PLAY IN THE FOLLOWING MANNER:

1) Move from the joint CLOSEST TO THE WRIST, independent of the other fingers.
2) Stay OUTSIDE AND TO THE LEFT of the " i-m-a" fingers.
3) When finished with the REST stroke, the thumb rests against the following string.
4) When finished with the FREE stroke (next page), it rests against the "i" finger.

Leaving fingers "i-m-a" in IN POSITION, play the thumb notes below. Move the thumb from string to string, as required, BUT KEEP IT IN POSITION. Use **REST STROKE.**

1

NOW, POSITION THE THUMB ON STRING 5 AND LEAVE IT THERE.

WITH ALL FINGERS IN PLACE, play the "i" finger only, pushing it back as if you were "scratching" the string. After the "i" finger has played string 3, you will notice that it is not resting on string 4, but positioned FREELY ABOVE IT. This is the **FREE STROKE.** Take

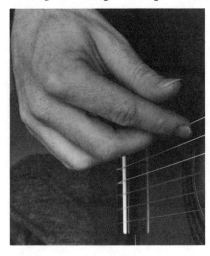

a look at these pictures. Contrast the picture at left (FREE stroke finish) with that on the right (REST stroke finish).

Play the "i" finger again. It's on string 3. Be sure all other fingers are still in their appointed places. Now, after you have played the "i" finger, **PREPARE** it for the next note by placing is back ON STRING 3. Then play again. Follow this pattern of **PLAY - PREPARE - PLAY - PREPARE** until it is automatic.

play prepare play prepare   etc.

FOLLOW THE SAME PROCEDURE IN TRAINING THE "m" FINGER.

NOW TEACH THE "a" FINGER.

NEXT, play the "i-m-a" fingers one after another. **KEEP EACH FINGER ON ITS APPOINTED STRING UNTIL IT PLAYS.** This is a vital portion of this technique lesson. After all three fingers have played, **PREPARE THEM ALL AT ONCE BY PLACING THEM BACK ON THE PROPER STRINGS.**

REPEAT THIS EXERCISE UNTIL THE FINGERS PREPARE THEMSELVES AUTOMATICALLY AND CORRECTLY AFTER EACH PLAYING.

FINALLY, you may play all three fingers AND the thumb in the same measure. Now, however, you will need to PREPARE ALL FOUR after they have played. Be very careful to get this right. Your future playing speed may well depend upon it.

1) when "p" plays, "i-m-a" prepare
2) when "a" plays, "p" prepares
3) use free stroke with all fingers

Now try a line where the thumb changes notes.

This line does not give you a rest for preparing the fingers, but by now you will be able to do it as a matter of course. If not, practice until you can.

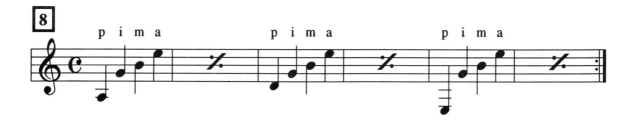

NOTATION OF CHORDS YOU ALREADY KNOW

You now have all the technical tools to play **ARPEGGIOS. AN ARPEGGIO IS A CHORD IN WHICH THE NOTES ARE PLAYED ONE AFTER ANOTHER** in any order chosen by the composer. An arpeggio is sometimes referred to as a **BROKEN CHORD.**

The Am chord diagram is shown below. If you were to play all six notes of Am, one after another, it would look like the notation given.

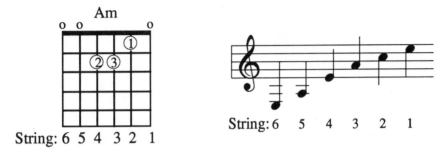

Since you are using only four right hand fingers, play just the notes below. DON'T FORGET TO PREPARE AFTER PLAYING ALL FOUR NOTES.

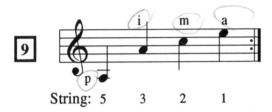

The E chord, with four notes selected from the six possible, looks like this:

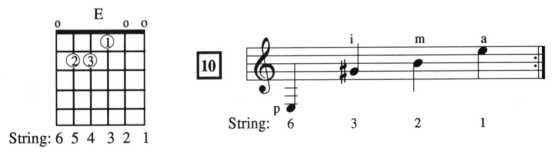

Notice that we are using the "p" finger to play the ROOT of each chord and the "i-m-a" fingers are playing ONLY THOSE NOTES FOUND ON STRINGS 3, 2 AND 1. Use left hand fingerings provided.

Learn the notes for the Dm chord now.

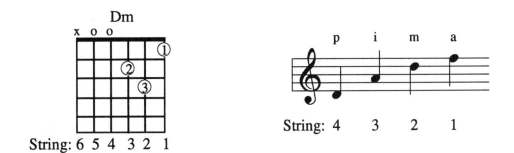

PLAY THE FOLLOWING EXERCISES. PLEASE DON'T SKIP ANY AND STAY WITH EACH ONE UNTIL IT SOUNDS AND FEELS FLUENT. Arabic numbers above the notes indicate left hand finger usage.

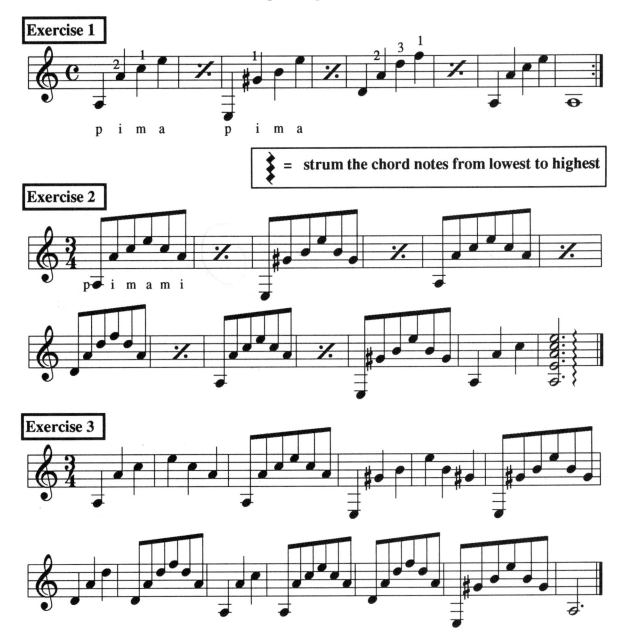

PLAYING BLOCK CHORDS WITH THE "i-m-a" FINGERS

Now, instead of playing the "i-m-a" fingers one at a time in arpeggio style, pluck all three at once in a sort of triple-headed free stroke. **KEEP THUMB IN POSITION.** The chord is given for each measure of notation.

Exercise 4

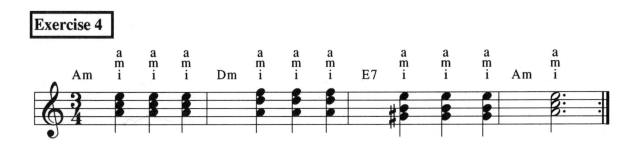

In the next exercise, add a bass note played with the thumb.

Exercise 5

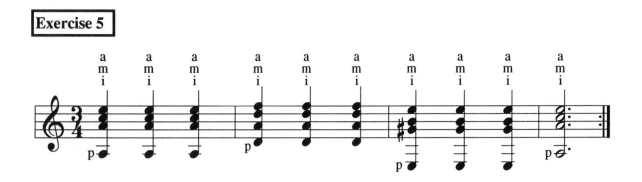

In this exercise you will combine block chords, arpeggios and thumb use.

Exercise 6

USING OTHER CHORDS IN ARPEGGIO STYLE PLAYING.

Measure numbers have been added to assist your practice. They appear below the treble clef at the beginning of each line of music.

TRIPLET EIGHTH NOTES

The beat note (note receiving one beat) may be subdivided in different ways. In the music you have played so far:

two eighth notes = one quarter

However, it is also possible to notate TRIPLETS, three eighth notes connected by a beam and having a "3" placed above or below them. These also equal one quarter note.

triplet eighth notes = one quarter

Below are some examples of measures using contrasting beat subdivisions of the quarter note. Count them carefully. **KEEP THE QUARTER NOTE BEAT CONSTANT WHEN PLAYING THESE LINES.**

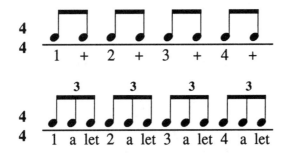

Play the following arpeggio exercise, using triplet eighth notes. USE CORRECT RIGHT HAND FINGERS: "p - i - m". Notice that only the triplets found in the first measure have been labeled with the "3". This is standard practice and indicates that the beamed eighth note groups which follow are also triplet eighths.

p i m p i m p i m etc.

TWO ARPEGGIO SOLOS FOR PRACTICE AND/OR PERFORMANCE

UNIT SEVEN

TABLATURE

TABLATURE is a very old way of writing music for stringed instruments. It is still used extensively today, especially in folk, bluegrass and rock styles. In rock, for instance, it is essential to know both tablature AND standard notation in order to correctly play much current printed music.

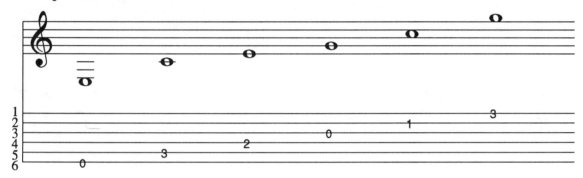

The representation above shows **GUITAR TABLATURE beneath a line of standard notation**. The six horizontal lines represent the six guitar strings. The string numbers are given at the left side of the diagram. The numbers appearing ON THE LINES represent the FRET on which you will place your left hand finger to produce the note desired. For instance: o = open string, 2 = second fret, 3 = third fret. **THIS TABLATURE DOES NOT TELL YOU WHICH LEFT HAND FINGER TO USE.**

DO WORK SHEET 10, page 118.

DEFINING THE RHYTHM IN TABLATURE is very simple. It looks much like the notation you already read. Study the examples below. **The first line is tablature. The second is a representation of the same pitches in standard notation.** Notice that there are two methods of writing the dotted half note in tablature form (ties may also be used to write half or whole notes).

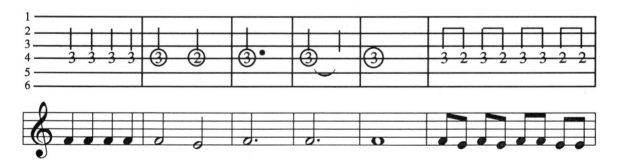

DO WORK SHEET 11, page 119.

PLAYING TECHNIQUES

HAMMERING ON (*ligado*)

The hammering technique (also called *ligado*) is used in most, if not all, styles of guitar music. To get started playing the hammer-on, follow the instructions and examples below.

THE HAMMER-ON IS USED TO PLAY THE SECOND OF TWO DIFFERENT PITCHES CONNECTED BY A CURVED LINE CALLED A **SLUR.** (A tie looks much the same as a slur; however, the tie connects two pitches which are IDENTICAL.)

IN EACH CASE, THE SECOND PITCH IS HIGHER THAN THE FIRST.
  1) Pluck the first pitch with a right hand finger or the pick.
  2) Sound the second, HIGHER pitch by HAMMERING-ON A GIVEN FINGER OF THE LEFT HAND. To get a good sound from pitch 2, hammer the finger with some velocity (about what you would need to depress a key on an old-fashioned manual typewriter). Try these examples.

a) Pluck the open G string with right hand to sound the G.
b) WHILE THE STRING IS STILL VIBRATING, hammer left hand finger 1 on the first fret of string 3 to sound G♯.

a) Pluck the open G.
b) Hammer left hand finger 2 at fret 2 of the G string to sound the A.

a) Place left hand finger 1 on fret 1, string 1. Pluck with the right hand to sound F.
b) Hammer left hand finger 3 on fret 3, string 1 to sound G.

PLAY THE FOLLOWING EXERCISES.

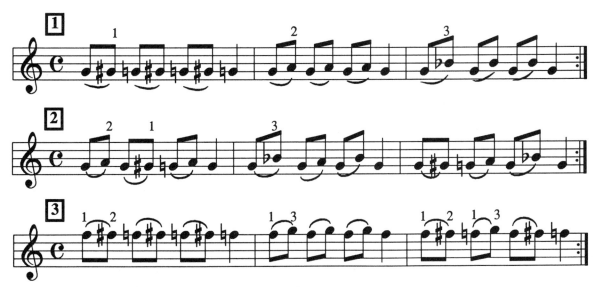

THE PULL-OFF

The pull-off is exactly the opposite of the hammer-on. That is, THE SECOND PITCH IS ALWAYS LOWER THAN THE FIRST. To play the example:

1) Place left hand finger 2 on the FIRST NOTE (A). SOUND THIS PITCH BY PLUCKING WITH THE RIGHT HAND.

2) Sound the second note (G) by PLUCKING STRING 3 (open G) WITH FINGER 2 OF THE LEFT HAND. This finger is already placed on the string at fret 2. Simply draw it back toward the palm to sound the G.

Pick   pull-off

In the pull-off notation below, the second pitch is NOT AN OPEN STRING. Therefore, BOTH FINGERS OF THE LEFT HAND MUST BE IN PLACE BEFORE SOUNDING THE FIRST PITCH. To play:

1) Place left hand finger 1 on the "C" and finger 3 on "D". Sound the "D" by plucking with the right hand.

2) Sound the "C" by pulling off with left hand finger 3 already in place on the string.

Pick   pull-off

THE SLIDE

To execute this technique, sound the first note (A) by plucking with the right hand. SLIDE the left hand to the position designated for the second note (B). DON'T PLUCK THE SECOND NOTE.

Pick   slide

Use a flatpick when playing this old folk tune. Use down (⊓) and up (∨) strokes as shown.

ARKANSAS TRAVELER

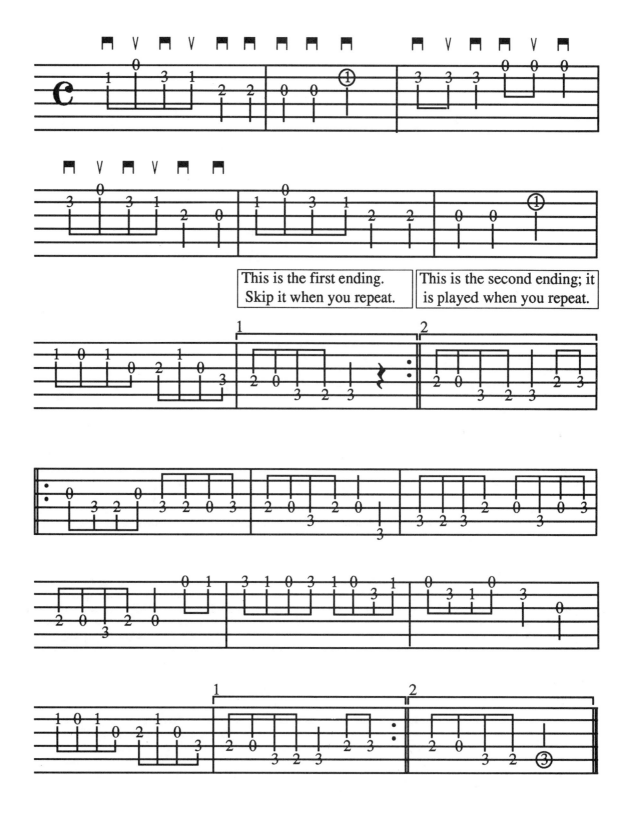

This is the first ending. Skip it when you repeat.

This is the second ending; it is played when you repeat.

74

Our version of this old tune uses hammers, pull-offs, slides and three-note chords.

WILDWOOD FLOWER

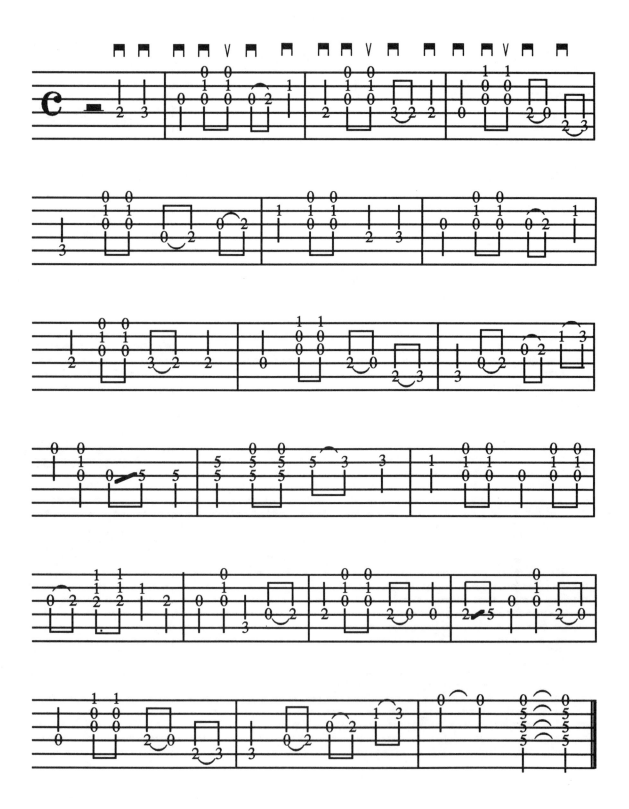

UNIT EIGHT

NATURAL NOTES, FRETS 1-12

From your study of barre chords you already understand all the names of the notes on strings 6 and 5. As you were able to find all these pitches by counting half and whole steps from the open position, you will find it easy to do the same thing on the other four strings.

WITHOUT WORRYING ABOUT NOTATION, FIND ALL THE NATURAL NOTES FROM "OPEN" TO FRET 12 ON EACH OF THE SIX STRINGS. REMEMBER: THE HALF-STEPS ARE FOUND AT B - C AND E - F.

Here is a simple chart showing you the natural notes for the full fretboard. You can figure out the sharps and flats for yourself.

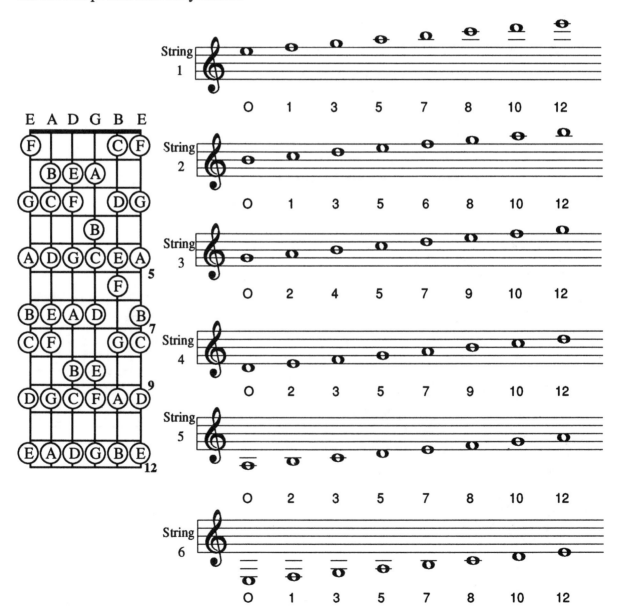

POSITION PLAYING

You have probably noticed that most pitches may be found in more than one place on the fingerboard. How do you know which one to play?

This is a complicated question, but there are at least two major considerations. First your POSITION will depend upon the notation of the piece. If the melody contains notes above fret 4, you will need to move out of first position. The position you use depends on the pitches in the tune. A second reason for playing a note in a given position is the TIMBRE (TONE QUALITY) you desire for that note.

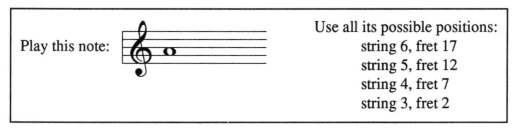

Play this note:

Use all its possible positions:
string 6, fret 17
string 5, fret 12
string 4, fret 7
string 3, fret 2

LISTEN FOR THE VARIETY IN TIMBRE.

THE DIAGRAM BELOW IS A POSITION SCALE. NOTICE THAT THE FRETBOARD HAS BEEN LEFT OPEN ON THE TOP AND BOTTOM OF THE DIAGRAM. THAT IS BECAUSE THIS SCALE IS MOVABLE.

THE LOWEST KEYNOTE FOR A MAJOR SCALE IS ENCLOSED IN A SQUARE.
(The diamond encloses the keynote for the relative minor scale.)

1) **BEGIN PLAYING ON THE MAJOR KEYNOTE.**
2) Learn just one string at a time.
3) Keep a perfect fingering at all times.
4) Check position for both hands.
5) Learn the scale ASCENDING ONLY.
6) Play the pitches with a) right thumb, then
   b) i-m alternation
7) Play quarter notes, then eighth notes
8) NOW, YOU MAY GO BACKWARD.
9) When you play the descending scale, GO ALL THE WAY PAST THE LOWEST MAJOR KEYNOTE TO THE BOTTOM PITCH, then come back up and end on the **keynote.**
10) Play this scale at 5th position, then move it around to 7th, 9th, 3rd.

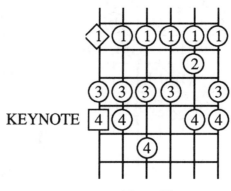

KEYNOTE

Figure 32

DO WORK SHEETS 12 AND 13, pages 120 and 121.

FIFTH POSITION

If the previously learned movable scale is placed in FIFTH POSITION, is looks like this:

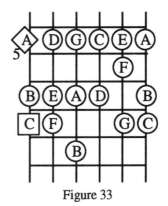

Figure 33

NOTATION FOR THIS SCALE IS SHOWN BELOW.

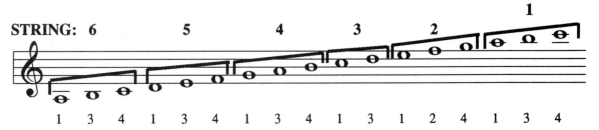

STRING: 6   5   4   3   2   1

1 3 4 1 3 4 1 3 4 1 3 1 2 4 1 3 4

Following are several melodies to play in fifth position. **WRITE IN THE COUNTING.**

UNIT NINE
TRANSPOSITION

Most of the music of the Western world is based on one of the major or minor scales and is therefore in a KEY. The musician sometimes finds it necessary to move the song upward or downward from its original key (usually done to facilitate performance). This is called **TRANSPOSITION.** In your song section you will find the music to "Buffalo Gals". It is written in the key of C. If you find this key too high for your singing voice, you may move it downward to a lower key. If it is too low, you may move upward.

Transposition is simple if you follow the procedure below and use the transposition chart on the next page. On that chart you will see that each major scale is spelled out and that its pitches are in seven columns. In the key of C, for instance, the I note is C, the ii note is D. In the key of D, the I note is D and the ii note is E.

On each pitch of the scale, a chord may be built. These chords are our concern in transposing the RHYTHM GUITAR PART of a lead sheet. Use the following procedure:

1) Find the key of your song.
2) Locate that scale on the chart.
3) Choose your new key.
4) Locate the new scale on the chart.
5) Beside or below the chord names of the old key, place the chord names of the new key. **USE LETTER NAMES EXACTLY AS ON THE CHART. IF A SHARP OR FLAT APPEARS BESIDE A LETTER, IT MUST BE USED.**
6) Finally, transfer the chord quality. (Quality refers to the kind of chord to be played: major, minor, diminished, augmented, seventh, minor seventh, etc.)

Below are the D and F scales as they appear on your transposition chart. Assume that D is your old key and F is the one to which you will transpose.

I	ii	iii	IV	V	vi	vii
D	E	F♯	G	A	B	C♯
F	G	A	B♭	C	D	E

EXAMPLE 1:	If your song is in the key of D			
	and the chords used are:	D	G	A
	You transpose to F by using:	F	B♭	C

EXAMPLE 2:	In the key of F:	Fmaj 7	Dm7	B♭ C9	F6	Am7♭5	C11
	In the key of D:	Dmaj7	Bm7	G A9	D6	F♯m7♭5	A11
	In the key of C:	Cmaj 7	Am7	F G9	C6	Em7♭5	G11

DO WORK SHEET 14, page 122.

TRANSPOSITION CHART

Upper case letters indicate major chords; lower case show minor or diminished chords.

KEY	I	ii	iii	IV	V	vi	vii
C	C	d	e	F	G	a	b
C#	C#	d#	e#	F#	G#	a#	b#
D	D	e	f#	G	A	b	c#
E♭	E♭	f	g	A♭	B♭	c	d
E	E	f#	g#	A	B	c#	d#
F	F	g	a	B♭	C	d	e
F#	F#	g#	a#	B	C#	d#	e#
G♭	G♭	a♭	b♭	C♭	D♭	e♭	f
G	G	a	b	C	D	e	f#
A♭	A♭	b♭	c	D♭	E♭	f	g
A	A	b	c#	D	E	f#	g#
B♭	B♭	c	d	E♭	F	g	a
B	B	c#	d#	E	F#	g#	a#

UNIT TEN

PLAYING THE BLUES

The blues form is an important part of the American musical heritage. The 12-bar blues is shown here. There are other forms. (Note: measure and bar mean the same thing.)

USING THE CHART BELOW, PLAY THE 12-BAR BLUES IN THE KEY OF E. USE A STRAIGHT DOWN STRUM. MEMORIZE THE PATTERN. (Review page 7 concerning the meaning of I, IV and V7.)

PATTERN: I   IV   I   V7   IV   I

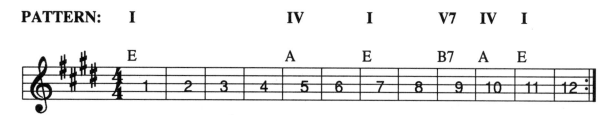

When playing through more than once (as in several verses of a song) the last two measures may be played:

USING ONLY THE E CHORD, PLAY THE BLUES STRUM BELOW WITH YOUR FLAT PICK. THE DIAGRAM CONSTRASTS THE NEW BLUES STRUM (a triplet form) WITH THE **STRAIGHT** ONE YOU'VE BEEN USING.

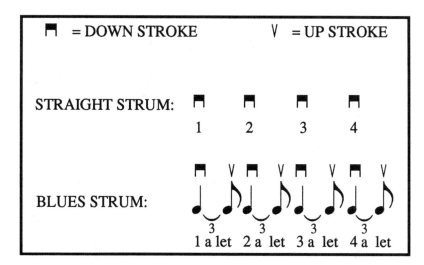

When your right hand is steady, add the A and B7 chords, following the basic 12-bar formula learned previously.

ADDING NOTES TO THE BLUES PROGRESSION

Notes may be added to each chord as shown. Each chord diagram represents one beat, all four of them constituting ONE measure of the designated chord.

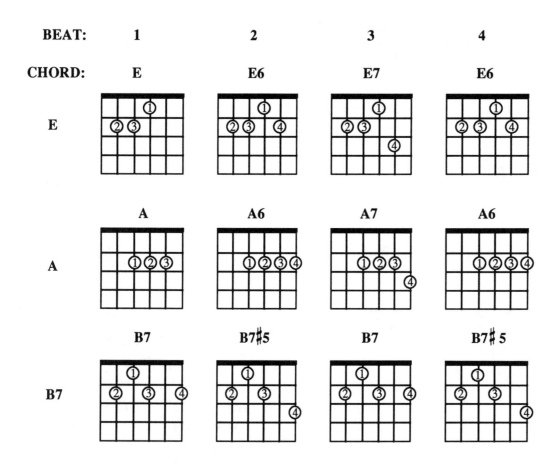

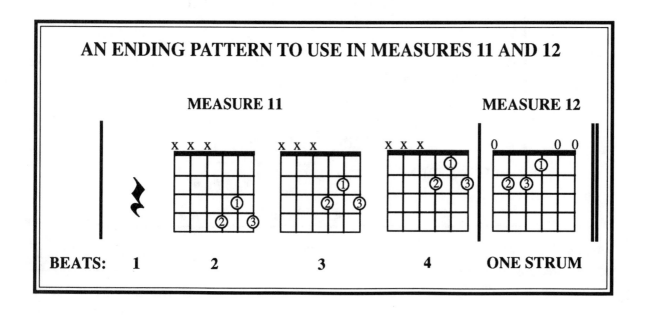

ADDING A HAMMER-ON TO THE BLUES PATTERN

To create a distinctive "blues" sound, try the following steps to add a hammer-on technique to what you already know. (If you have not yet done the hammer-on section of the book, refer to page 71 now for instructions.)

USE THE "E" CHORD FOR PRACTICE. PLAY EACH STEP UNTIL IT IS SMOOTH.

1) THIS IS THE STRUM YOU ALREADY KNOW

　　　⊓　V ⊓　V ⊓　V ⊓　V
　　　1 a let 2 a let 3 a let 4 a let

2) NEXT, LEAVE BEAT ONE SILENT, BUT KEEP THE REST OF THE PATTERN THE SAME. Move the pick or thumb down as you normally would on beat one; just don't let it hit any strings.

　　　𝄾　V ⊓　V ⊓　V ⊓　V
　　　1 a let 2 a let 3 a let 4 a let

3) When you play the "let" after "4," LIFT YOUR LEFT HAND OFF THE CHORD, PLAYING ALL STRINGS OPEN.

　　　　　　　　　　　　strum
　　　　　　　　　　　　open
　　　𝄾　V ⊓　V ⊓　V ⊓　V
　　　1 a let 2 a let 3 a let 4 a let

4) Finally, hammer the full chord back on the fretboard on beat 1, while your right hand is "missing" the strings.

　　hammer　　　　　　strum
　　chord　　　　　　　open
　　　𝄾　V ⊓　V ⊓　V ⊓　V
　　　1 a let 2 a let 3 a let 4 a let

THIS IS NOT A SIMPLE PATTERN, SO BE PATIENT WITH YOURSELF.

When it seems smooth using the E chord, try it with A and B7. Next, see if you can do it with the entire 12-bar formula. The final step is to apply this technique to any blues song you enjoy.

UNIT ELEVEN

ADDITIONAL RHYTHM MATERIALS

RIGHT HAND STRUMMING PATTERNS

You know the straight down strum, the root-strum pattern, the root-fifth strum pattern and a basic blues strum. Here are more strums to add to your accompaniment skills. When you have learned these, try your hand at developing some new ones. Apply any of them to your favorite songs.

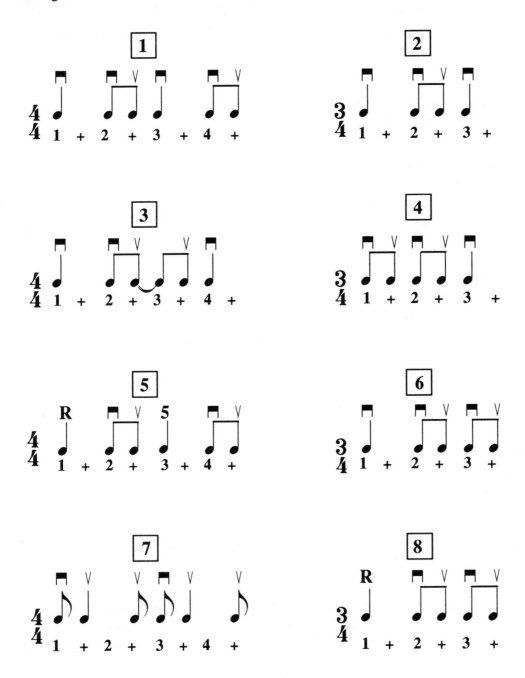

ADDITIONAL RHYTHM GUITAR MATERIALS

LEARN ALL CHORDS IN THE MASTER CHART ON PAGE 87 by using them in the progressions given below. Some of these chords are actually short forms of the barre chord. They are very useful in both rhythm and solo playing. The diagrams illustrate how they are related to the barre. In each case, the pitches on strings 6 and 5 have been eliminated from play. Be sure to control the strum when playing these forms.

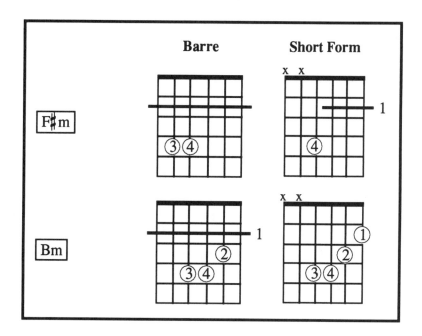

PROGRESSIONS FOR PRACTICE:

NOTE: M7 may also be written Maj7, Ma7 or 7.

1) A - AM7 - A7 - D - DM7 - D7 - G - GM7 - G7 - C - CM7 - C7 - F - FM7

2) D - Bm - Em - A7

3) A -F♯m - Bm - E7

4) Cm - Fm - G7

5) B♭m - Bm - Cm - C♯m

6) Fm - F♯m - Gm - G♯m

7) D - F♯m - G - A7

8) A - C♯m - D - E7

9) Bm - Em - F♯

10) Fm - B♭m - C7

THE DIMINISHED CHORD FORM:

The full four-note diminished chord form is shown at right. This chord is represented by the abbreviation "dim." or the "o" symbol: C dim. or C°. Each placement of this chord may carry four names, one for each pitch in the fingering. The chord at right, for instance, may be played for A dim., C dim., E♭ dim. or G♭ dim.

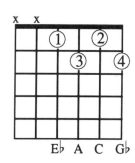

P - I - M - A ACCOMPANIMENT PATTERNS

Many combinations of the "p-i-m-a" pattern are possible. These, and others like them, are often used for accompanying melodies, as an alternative to strumming patterns. They are especially appropriate for ballads such as *Greensleeves* or *House of the Rising Sun*. The examples below are written for the *Am* chord form.

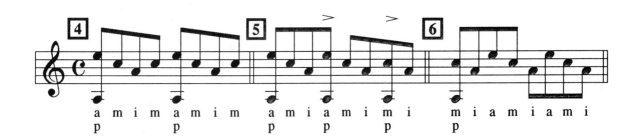

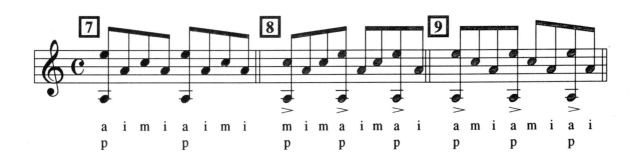

APPLY THESE PATTERNS APPROPRIATELY TO SONGS YOU ALREADY KNOW. THEN TRY CREATING PATTERNS OF YOUR OWN.

D bm, em A

Capo - 1. go down to easiest chord fingerings.
2. capo number of ½ steps that we went down.

written♭   play in
(3) E♭ = D capo 1
(4) A♭ = G capo 1
(2) B♭ = G capo 3
(6) F = D capo 3
(5) F♭ D♭ = C G capo 1

MASTER CHORD CHART

then p80 trans- position chart

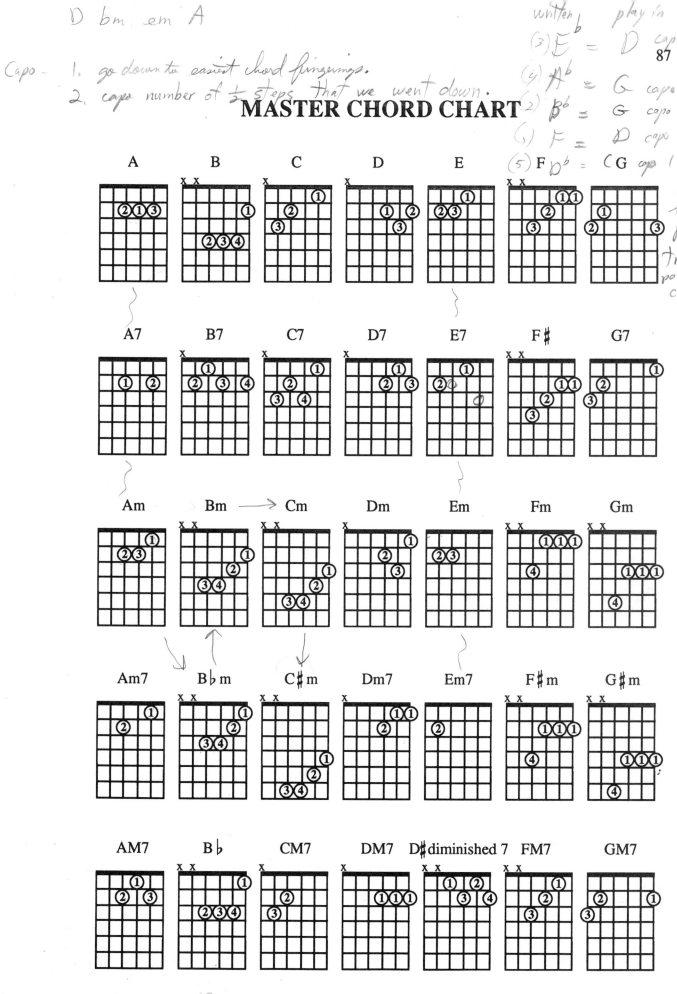

A B C D E F# G

A7 B7 C7 D7 E7 F# G7

Am Bm → Cm Dm Em Fm Gm

Am7 B♭m C#m Dm7 Em7 F#m G#m

AM7 B♭ CM7 DM7 D# diminished 7 FM7 GM7

Bar

UNIT TWELVE

THE 6/8 TIME SIGNATURE

6   means   **6**   beats per measure

8   means   ♪ receives one beat

Here are some basic note values in 6/8 time. **LEARN THEM.**

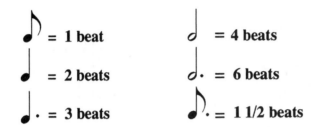

>   is an **ACCENT**
Play this note a little stronger.

PLAY THESE 6/8 MELODIES.

HERE ARE TWO FAMILIAR TUNES IN 6/8 TIME. WRITE IN THE COUNTING AND
PLAY THEM. Notice that the "Greensleeves" melody, which you played previously in 3/4
time, can also be notated in this meter. It will sound the same, whichever notation is used.

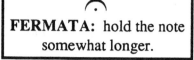

FERMATA: hold the note somewhat longer.

WE THREE KINGS

GREENSLEEVES

UNIT THIRTEEN

ROCK GUITAR TECHNIQUE: POWER CHORDS

Power chords are two-note chords most often heard in rock music, especially punk and hard rock. They are also found in country, blues and other styles. When played on an electric guitar with a loud amplifier set to a distorted tone, they sound quite powerful. The nickname may have come from this sound.

The two notes needed to form any power chord are a **ROOT** and **FIFTH**. You learned the relationship of these two notes in Unit Three. The naming of power chords is simple: the name says it all. **C5**: the **root is C** and the other note in the chord is the **fifth** note of the C major scale. **A♭5**: the root is **A♭** and the other note is the **fifth** note of the A♭ major scale.

Create the F5 power chord by placing the first finger of your left hand in fret one of string six. This is the root note: F. To find the fifth, place your third finger on fret three of string five. Strum only strings 6 and 5. Move to C5, strumming only strings 5 and 4. The fingering is the same for these and all power chords.

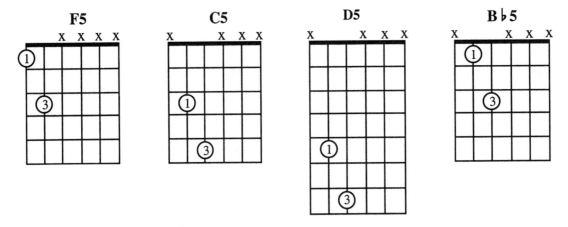

Control the pick while strumming. Do not strum any strings with "**x**" placed above them. Notice that the strummed strings are **only** those fingered by the left hand. Play exercise 1, using the chords above.

Play the line again in example 2 on the next page. This time, use a **heavy** right thumb or pick attack. To bring out the power of these power chords, use all down strums.

☐ = down strum

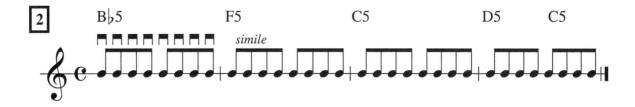

Learn the E5, F#5 and G5 power chords shown below. Notice that they include a third note played by finger 4. This note is another root, therefore the name of the chord is not altered. With this additional note, the power chord sounds fuller and louder. Play exercise 3.

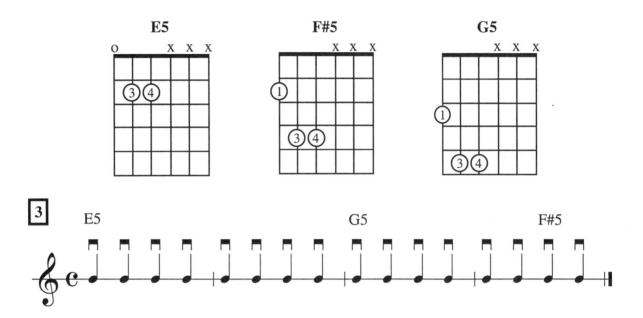

Another right hand technique often used in conjunction with power chords is **palm muting**. This technique involves placing the right side of your palm on the bridge and strings in order to dampen the strings being strummed. When used properly, it allows the guitarist to diminish the volume of some notes and accentuate others.

To get started with palm muting, align the right side of your palm on the bridge and touch all six strings at the same time. In this position you will achieve a medium palm muting effect. Examine the photo at the right.

To create a more heavily muted, "chunky" sound, slide your strumming hand toward the neck a half-inch or so, taking on more of the strings. To create a light, subtle muting effect do the opposite: move the palm more toward the bridge and dampen less string.

92

In the following line, palm mute the E5, F#5 and G5 power chords. Slightly reposition your strumming hand on the bridge by moving it toward your body about an inch. This allows you to strum strings 6, 5 and 4 comfortably AND maintain the muting. (In this case we do not need to mute strings 3, 2 and 1.)

Play example 4 with three different degrees of muting: medium, heavy and light. Do this by taking on more or less of the strings, as explained on the previous page.

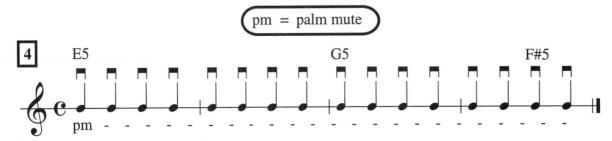

In example 5 accentuate beats three and four of measures two and four by simply lifting your palm mute off the strings momentarily. Pick as usual. This will cause the strings to ring normally, sounding much louder than the palm muted chords. Use heavy palm mute.

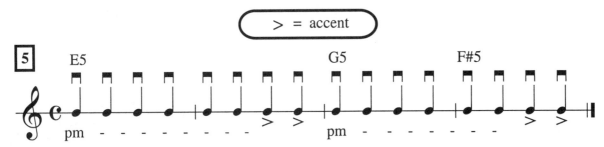

In this final line, combine several of the above techniques. Begin with heavy palm muting. In measures 3-4 gradually reduce the palm mute by sliding the palm toward the bridge, as shown in the score. Use the chord frames on pp. 90 and 91 as a reference for finding the new chords. Position the G5 power chord. Move one fret toward the bridge for G#5 and another fret for A5. Move C5 appropriately to find C#5 and B5.

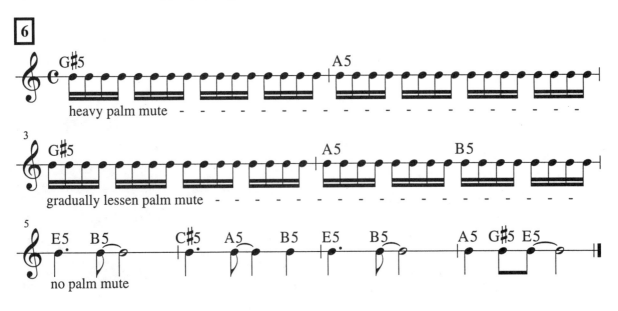

POWER CHORD BLUES

In Unit One you played the 12-bar blues with regular chords. We will now further our study of power chords by applying them to this blues form and to early 50's rock styles. The chart below indicates one possible chord change format for the 12-bar blues.

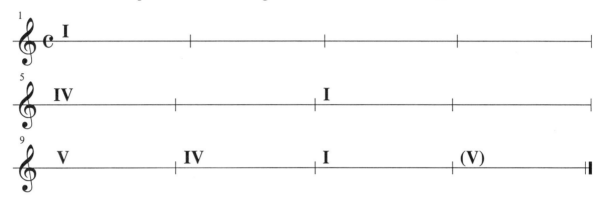

In each of the two patterns below, one-measure samples are provided for the I, IV and V chords. Apply the samples to the 12-bar format above. Playing them with straight eighths tends to sound more like the 50's rock style of Chuck Berry, while swing eighths evoke the blues shuffle feel. Try both styles.

Blues Pattern #1

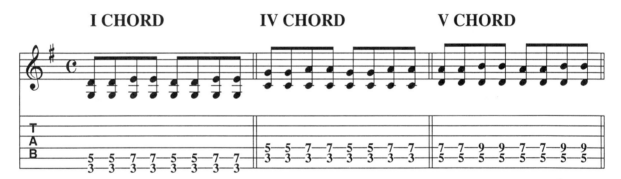

In Pattern #2, keep the 1st and 3rd fingers "locked" in the power chord position and play all the moving notes with left hand finger 4.

Blues Pattern #2

Worried Man

Traditional

It takes a wor- ried man to sing a wor- ried song. It takes a wor- ried man to sing a wor- ried song. It takes a wor- ried man to sing a wor- ried song. I'm wor- ried now, but I won't be wor- ried long.

Crawdad Song

Traditional

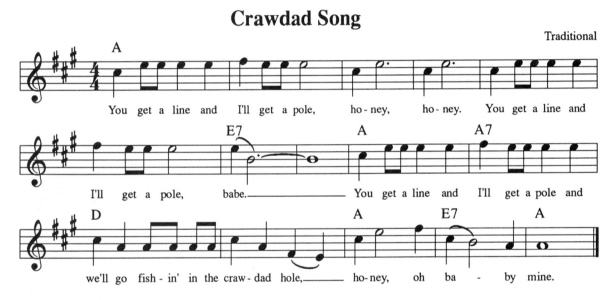

You get a line and I'll get a pole, ho - ney, ho - ney. You get a line and I'll get a pole, babe._____ You get a line and I'll get a pole and we'll go fish- in' in the craw- dad hole,_____ ho- ney, oh ba - by mine.

Gotta Travel On

Traditional

I've laid a- round and stayed a- round this old town too long. Sum- mer's al- most gone._____ Win- ter's com- in' on. I've laid a- round and stayed a- round this old town too long and it looks like I've got- ta tra- vel on.

Nobody Knows

Spiritual

No-bo-dy knows the trou-ble I've seen. No-bo-dy knows my sor-row.

No-bo-dy knows the trou-ble I've seen. Glo-ry hal-le-lu-jah. Some-times I'm up, some-

times I'm down. Oh yes, Lord. Some-times I'm al-most to the ground. Oh yes, Lord.

D.C. al Fine

Down by the Riverside

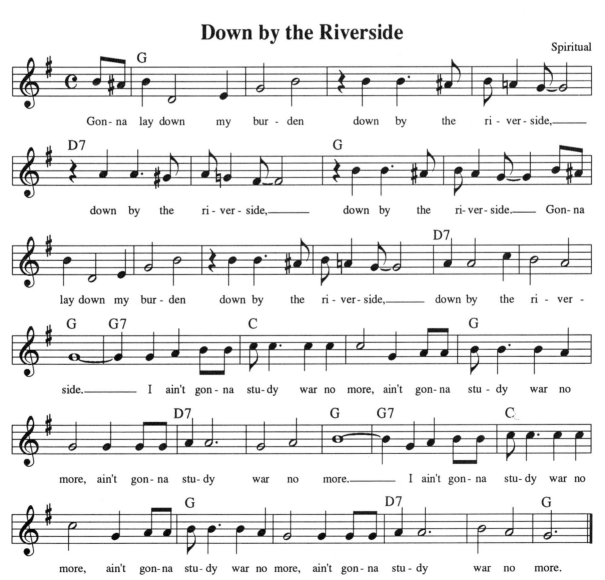

Spiritual

Gon-na lay down my bur-den down by the ri-ver-side,_____

down by the ri-ver-side,_____ down by the ri-ver-side._____ Gon-na

lay down my bur-den down by the ri-ver-side,_____ down by the ri-ver-

side._____ I ain't gon-na stu-dy war no more, ain't gon-na stu-dy war no

more, ain't gon-na stu-dy war no more._____ I ain't gon-na stu-dy war no

more, ain't gon-na stu-dy war no more, ain't gon-na stu-dy war no more.

When the Saints Go Marchin' In

Spiritual

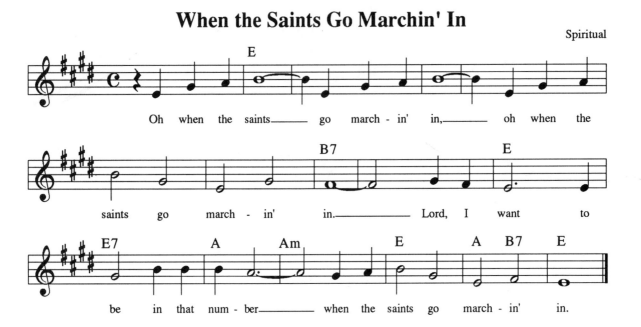

Oh when the saints go march-in' in, oh when the
saints go march-in' in. Lord, I want to
be in that num-ber when the saints go march-in' in.

The next song has MIXED METER. That is,
there is a change of time signature within the
song. Keep the quarter note beat constant
when going from 4/4 to 2/4 and back to 4/4.

Deep Blue Sea

Traditional

Deep blue sea, ba-by, deep blue sea. Deep blue sea, ba-by,
deep blue sea. Deep blue sea, ba-by, deep blue sea.
It was Wil-lie what got drownd-ed in the deep blue sea.

Shalom Chavarim

Greensleeves

Erie Canal

Traditional

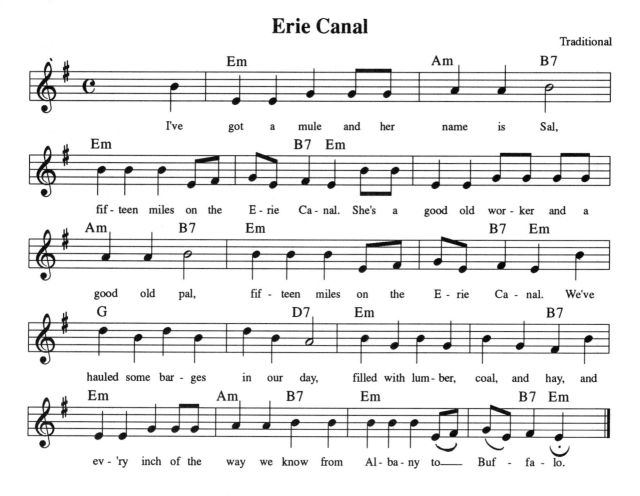

I've got a mule and her name is Sal, fif - teen miles on the E - rie Ca - nal. She's a good old wor - ker and a good old pal, fif - teen miles on the E - rie Ca - nal. We've hauled some bar - ges in our day, filled with lum - ber, coal, and hay, and ev - 'ry inch of the way we know from Al - ba - ny to— Buf - fa - lo.

Father's Whiskers

Traditional

We have a dear old fa - ther, for whom we dear - ly pray. He has a set of whis - kers. They're al - ways in the way. Oh, they're al - ways in the way. The cows eat them for hay. They hide the dirt on fa - ther's shirt, they're al - ways in the way.

500 Miles

Traditional

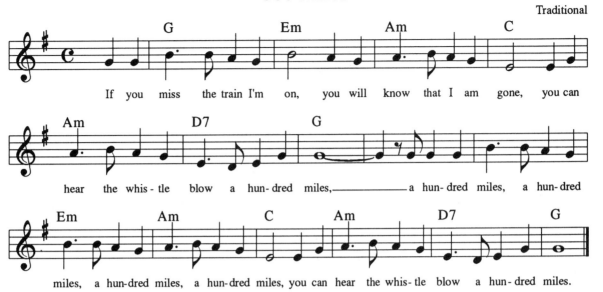

If you miss the train I'm on, you will know that I am gone, you can

hear the whis-tle blow a hun-dred miles,———a hun-dred miles, a hun-dred

miles, a hun-dred miles, a hun-dred miles, you can hear the whis-tle blow a hun-dred miles.

Notice that there is a key change in the middle of this song. The sharp is cancelled for the remainder of the tune.

House of the Rising Sun

Traditional

Joshua

Spiritual

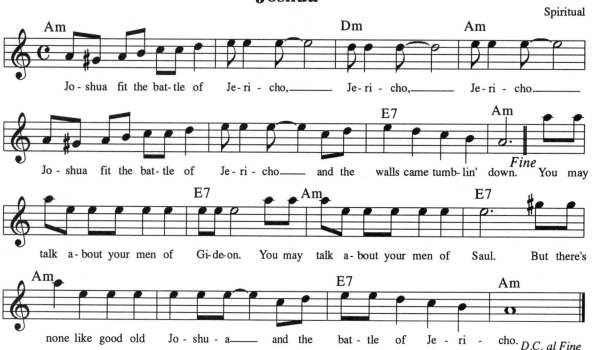

Jo - shua fit the bat - tle of Je - ri - cho,____ Je - ri - cho,____ Je - ri - cho.____

Jo - shua fit the bat - tle of Je - ri - cho____ and the walls came tumb - lin' down. You may

talk a - bout your men of Gi - de - on. You may talk a - bout your men of Saul. But there's

none like good old Jo - shu - a____ and the bat - tle of Je - ri - cho. *D.C. al Fine*

Wayfaring Stranger

Spiritual

I'm just a poor____ way - far - in' stran - ger,____ a - trav' - lin' through____ this world of

woe;____ and there's no sick - ness, toil or dan - ger____ in that fair

land____ to which I go. I'm go - in' there____ to see my

moth - er;____ I'm go - in' there____ no more to roam.____ I'm just a -

go - in' o - ver Jor - dan.____ I'm just a - go - in' o - ver home.

Sakura

Traditional Japanese folk song

Sa - ku - ra, sa - ku - ra. Ya - yo - i no so - ra wa.

Mi - wa - ta - su ka - gi - ri. Ka - su - mi - ka ku - mo - ka. Ni - o - i - zo

i - zu - ru. I - za - ya, i - za - ya. Mi - ni yu - ka - n.

On Top of Old Smokey

Traditional

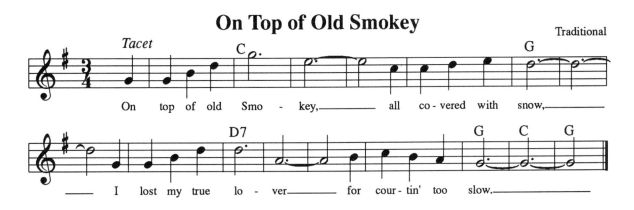

On top of old Smo - key,_____ all co - vered with snow,_____

_____ I lost my true lo - ver_____ for cour - tin' too slow._____

Rock-a My Soul

Spiritual

Rock - a my soul_____ in the bo - som of A - bra - ham, rock - a my soul___ in the

bo - som of A - bra - ham, rock - a my soul_____ in the

bo - som of A - bra - ham. Oh, rock - a my soul.

Comin' 'Round the Mountain

Traditional

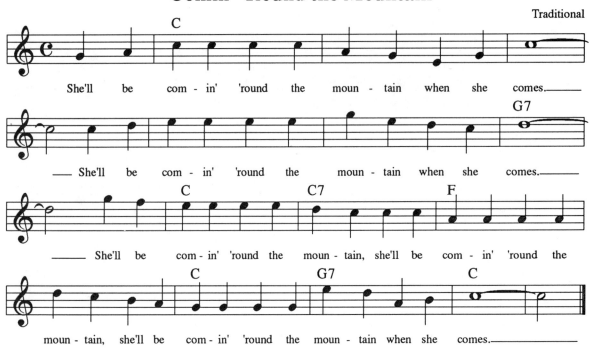

She'll be com - in' 'round the moun - tain when she comes.___

___ She'll be com - in' 'round the moun - tain when she comes.___

___ She'll be com - in' 'round the moun - tain, she'll be com - in' 'round the

moun - tain, she'll be com - in' 'round the moun - tain when she comes.___

Amazing Grace

Traditional

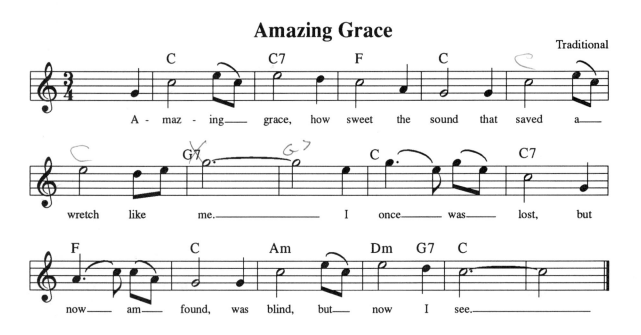

A - maz - ing___ grace, how sweet the sound that saved a___

wretch like me.___ I once___ was___ lost, but

now___ am___ found, was blind, but___ now I see.___

2. 'Twas grace that taught my heart to fear, and grace my fear relieved.
   How precious did that grace appear the hour I first believed.

3. Thru many dangers, toils and snares we have already come.
   'Twas grace that brought us safe thus far, and grace will bring us home.

4. When we've been there ten thousand years, bright shining as the sun,
   We've no less days to sing God's praise than when we first begun.

Buffalo Gals

Traditional

As I was walk-in' down the street, down the street,

down the street, a pret-ty gal I chanced to meet. Oh,

she was fair to see. Oh, buf-fa-lo gals won't you come out to-night,

come out to-night, come out to-night. Oh, buf-fa-lo gals, won't you

come out to-night and dance by the light of the moon.

Cielito Lindo

Traditional Folk Song

Cockles and Mussels

Traditional

In Dub-lin's fair ci-ty where girls are so pret-ty, 'twas there I first met my sweet Mol-ly Ma-lone. As she pushed her wheel-bar-row through streets broad and nar-row cry-ing cock-les and mus-sels a-live, a-live, oh. A-live, a-live, oh,___ a-live, a-live, oh,___ cry-ing cock-les and mus-sels a-live, a-live, oh.

Shenandoah

Traditional

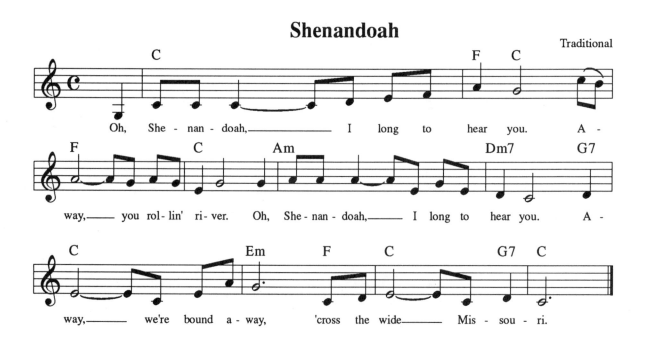

Oh, She-nan-doah,___ I long to hear you. A-way,___ you rol-lin' ri-ver. Oh, She-nan-doah,___ I long to hear you. A-way,___ we're bound a-way, 'cross the wide___ Mis-sou-ri.

The Huron Carol

Arr. Nancy Marsters

Canon

William Boyce (1710-1779)

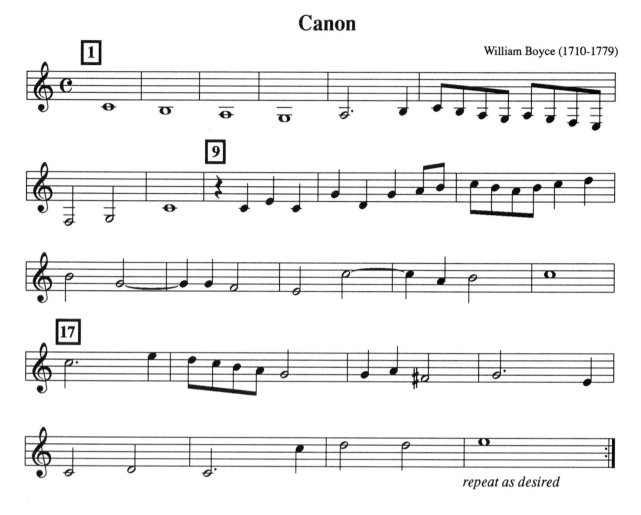

repeat as desired

PLAYING A CANON

The ***canon*** is a composition in which all performers play the same melody throughout the piece, beginning at different measures. A common term for canon is ***"round"***. The 24-measure canon above is written for three players and is performed in the following way:

1: Each player begins at the beginning of the tune and continues to the end, repeating for as long as the group designates; player 1 starts alone.

2: Player 2 begins when player 1 reaches measure 9.

3: Player 3 begins when player 1 reaches measure 17.

4: Performers commonly devise some suitable ending format.

Visit your library or media center for more information on William Boyce and other composers of this time period. Interesting information might include: 1) how the composer made a living during this time period, 2) how music was published and disseminated and 3) conventional performance venues available to music performers.

USEFUL MUSIC TERMINOLOGY

PITCH: highness or lowness of a **tone** (tones on the guitar are produced by the vibration of the strings)

DURATION: length of a tone

TIMBRE: tone quality

DYNAMICS: loudness or softness of a tone

COMMON MARKINGS

TERM	SYMBOL	MEANING
piano	p	soft
pianissimo	pp	very soft
mezzo piano	mp	medium soft
mezzo forte	mf	medium loud
forte	f	loud
fortissimo	ff	very loud
crescendo	cresc. or <	gradually louder
decrescendo	decresc. or >	gradually softer
diminuendo	dim.	gradually softer
sforzando	sfz	loud, then at once soft
ritardando	rit.	gradually slower
accelerando	accel.	gradually faster
fermata	⌢	hold
arpeggio	ξ	broken chord

OTHER MUSICAL SYMBOLS

accent (weakest to strongest)	— > ∧	play this note a little stronger
Da Capo al Fine	D. C. al Fine	go back to the beginning and play to Fine.
Dal Segno al Fine	D. S. al Fine	go back to the sign and play to Fine (the end)
Measure repeat		repeat previous measure

TEMPO MARKINGS

Tempo markings appear at the beginning of some pieces and indicate the general rate of speed of the music.

Largo	slow, stately
Adagio	slow
Andante	walking speed
Moderato	medium speed
Allegretto	not as fast as allegro
Allegro	lively, fast
Presto	quick

Other terms, when used alone or along with the tempo markings, indicate tempo and/or directions for proper performance.

Con brio	with spirit
Con moto	with movement
Cantabile	like singing (connected)
A tempo	return to original tempo

SPECIAL GUITAR SYMBOLS

1, 2, 3, 4	indicates fingering for the left hand
p, i, m, a	indicates fingering for the right hand
③, ⑤	play this note on string 3 (or string 5)
II, V (or pos II, pos V)	use position 2, position 5
C, ¢	barre, half-barre
CV, ¢III	barre at fret 5, half-barre at fret 3
pm - - - - - - - - -	palm mute

WORK SHEET 1 NAME _____

Name each note on the line provided below it.

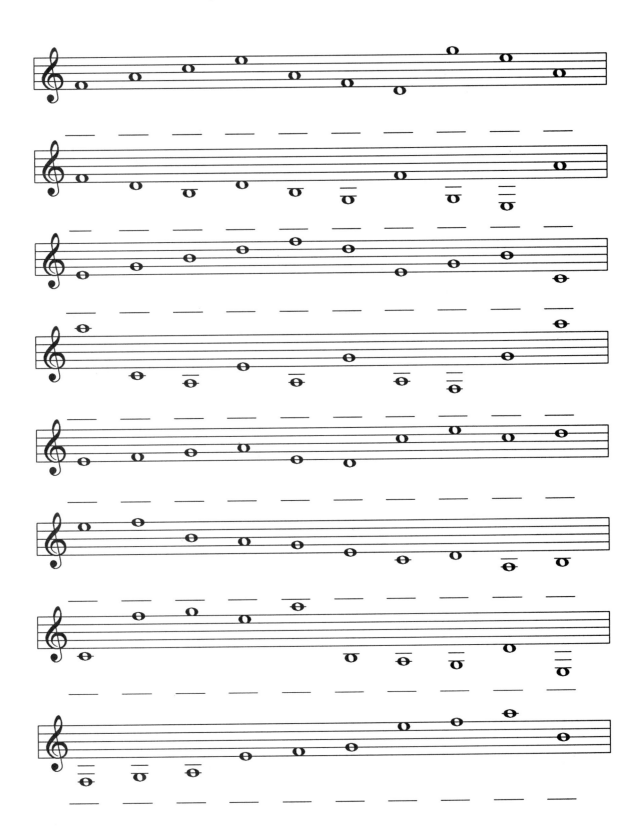

WORK SHEET 2   NAME _____

Write in the counting, following the example of the first line. Be sure that each number or "+" lies directly below the correct note or rest. Then, using any pitch, play each line while counting aloud.

USE A PENCIL.

WORK SHEET 3   NAME _____

Notate each diagrammed pitch in the correct measure below it. Use WHOLE NOTES.
Pitches 1 and 2 are notated as examples.

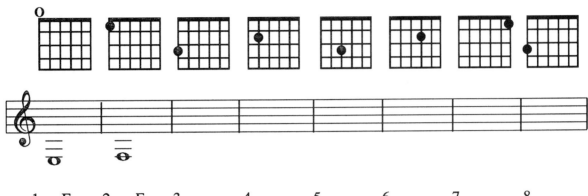

1 __E__   2 __F__   3 _____   4 _____   5 _____   6 _____   7 _____   8 _____

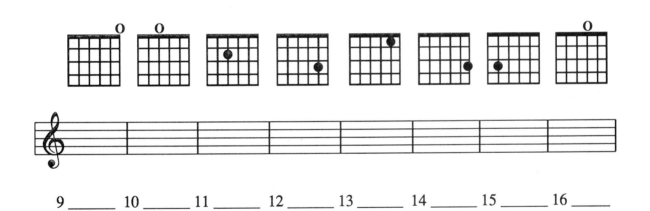

9 _____   10 _____   11 _____   12 _____   13 _____   14 _____   15 _____   16 _____

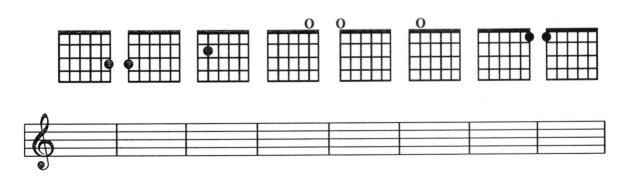

17 _____   18 _____   19 _____   20 _____   21 _____   22 _____   23 _____   24 _____

112

WORK SHEET 4　　　　　　**NAME** _____

Notate each diagrammed pitch (or pitches) in the correct measure below it. Some positions represent two pitches which are ENHARMONIC. WRITE THEM BOTH. Examples 1 and 2 are given.

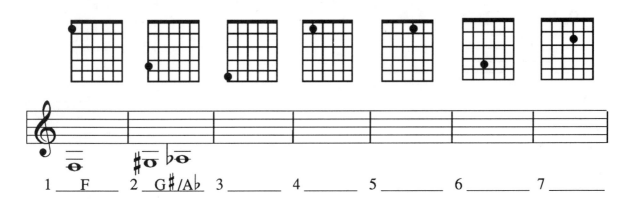

1 ___F___ 2 _G♯/A♭_ 3 _____ 4 _____ 5 _____ 6 _____ 7 _____

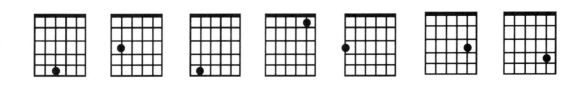

8 _____ 9 _____ 10 _____ 11 _____ 12 _____ 13 _____ 14 _____

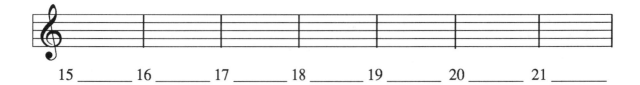

15 _____ 16 _____ 17 _____ 18 _____ 19 _____ 20 _____ 21 _____

WORK SHEET 5   NAME _____

Below are barre chord diagrams using movable
E chords. Use the following steps to name them:

1) Identify the chord beneath the barre. The example
   at right is Em.

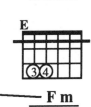

2) Place the ROOT NAME (E) above the E string and
   the CHORD QUALITY (m) on the answer line.

___ m

3) Identify the 6th string pitch on which the barre is
   found. This is the new ROOT NAME. Enter it on
   the answer line in front of the chord quality.

___ F m

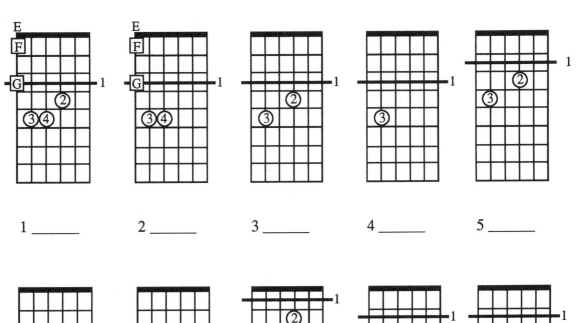

1 _____   2 _____   3 _____   4 _____   5 _____

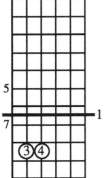   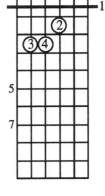   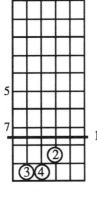   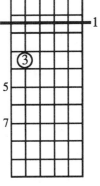   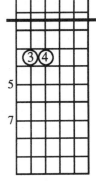

6 _____   7 _____   8 _____   9 _____   10 _____

114

WORK SHEET 6   NAME _____

Follow the same three-step procedure you used for work sheet 5. Recall that when you move "A" type chords, the root is always on string 5.

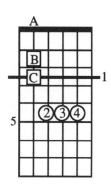

1 _____

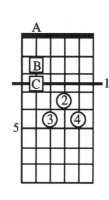

2 _____

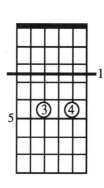

3 _____

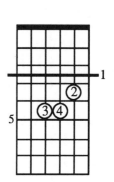

4 _____

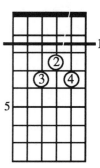

5 _____

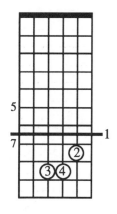

6 _____

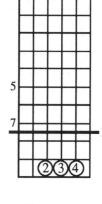

7 _____

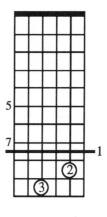

8 _____

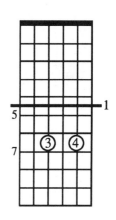

9 _____

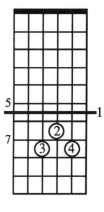

10 _____

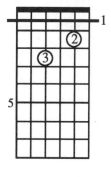

11 _____

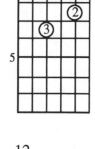

12 _____

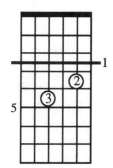

13 _____

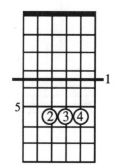

14 _____

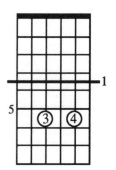

15 _____

WORK SHEET 7 NAME _____

This work sheet has both movable E and movable A chords. Be careful as you
FOLLOW THE CORRECT STEPS to find the name of the chord in each diagram.
Look at example 1. It is an A chord below the barre, so A has been written above
string 5. Example 2 is an Em7 below the barre, so the new root is on string 6.

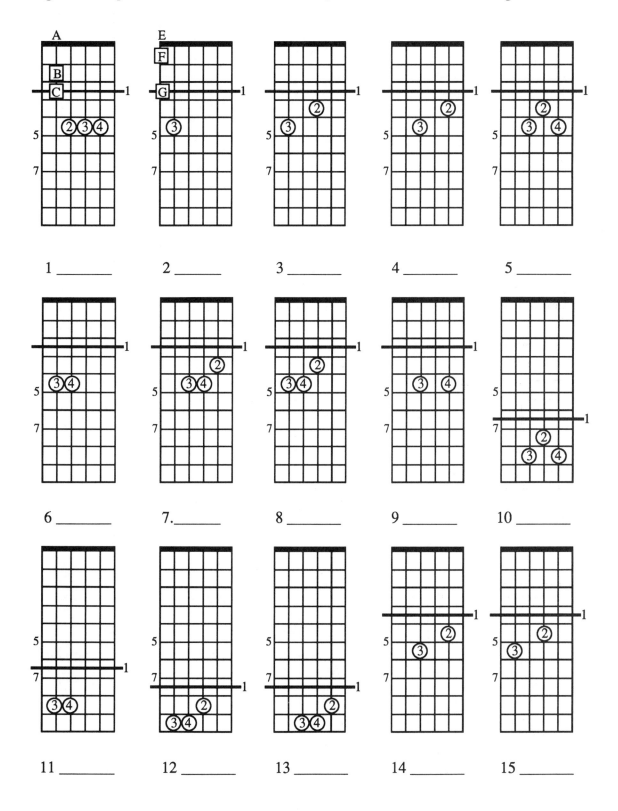

1 _____ 2 _____ 3 _____ 4 _____ 5 _____

6 _____ 7. _____ 8 _____ 9 _____ 10 _____

11 _____ 12 _____ 13 _____ 14 _____ 15 _____

WORK SHEET 8   NAME _____

Name each note on the lines provided. Then label the INTERVAL in each measure on the single lines marked "Label". Use the following designations:

H	=	half-step
W	=	whole step

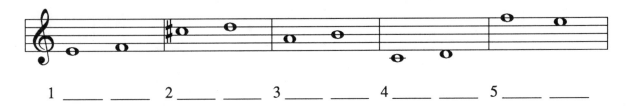

1 ____ ____   2 ____ ____   3 ____ ____   4 ____ ____   5 ____ ____

LABEL: ____   ____   ____   ____   ____

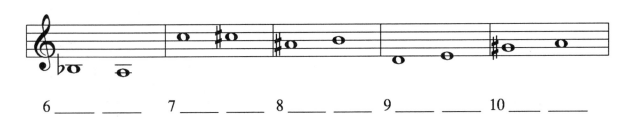

6 ____ ____   7 ____ ____   8 ____ ____   9 ____ ____   10 ____ ____

LABEL: ____   ____   ____   ____   ____

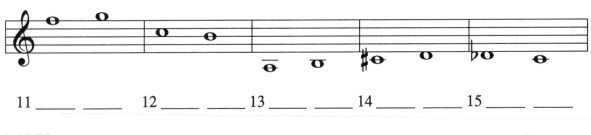

11 ____ ____   12 ____ ____   13 ____ ____   14 ____ ____   15 ____ ____

LABEL:____   ____   ____   ____   ____

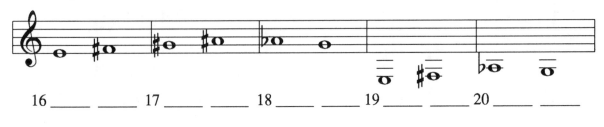

16 ____ ____   17 ____ ____   18 ____ ____   19 ____ ____   20 ____ ____

LABEL: ____   ____   ____   ____   ____

WORK SHEET 9　　　　　**NAME**_____

The seven flats always appear in key signatures IN THE SAME ORDER: B - E - A - D - G - C - F . As you will see in the flat signatures below, no matter how many flats appear in the key signature, they always come in this order. The correct method of writing them is shown below.

COPY THE SEVEN FLATS ON THE EMPTY STAVES PROVIDED. MEMORIZE.

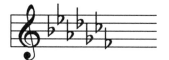　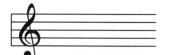　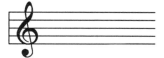

> **State the rule for finding the name of a flat key signature.**

NAME
EACH
KEY:
　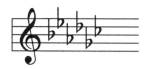　

THE ORDER OF SHARPS IS: F - C - G - D - A - E - B (helpful hint--these are the letter names of the flats in backward order). Copy the order of sharps on each staff.

　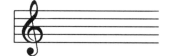　

> **State the rule for finding the name of each sharp key signature.**

WORK SHEET 10   NAME_____

**In the following exercises, notate each tablature pitch on the staff above it. If a pitch
has two notations which are enharmonic, write both (see examples 1 and 2).**

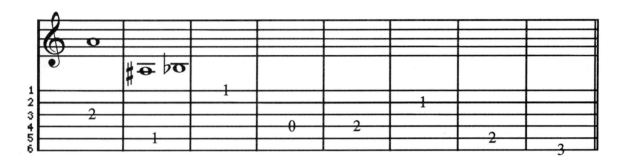

1 __A__   2 _A♯/B♭_ 3 _____ 4 _____ 5 _____ 6 _____ 7 _____ 8 _____

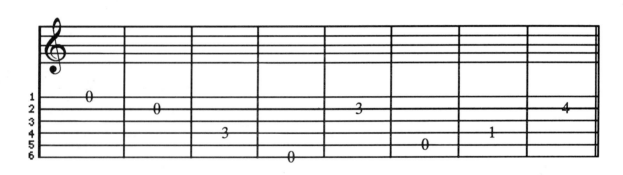

9 _____ 10 _____ 11 _____ 12 _____ 13_____ 14_____ 15_____ 16_____

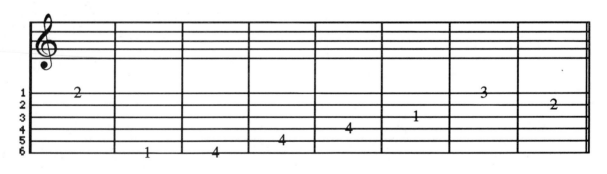

17_____ 18_____ 19_____ 20_____ 21_____ 22_____ 23_____ 24_____

WORK SHEET 11   **NAME** _____

Notate each tablature melody on the staff provided. **PLAY THEM.**

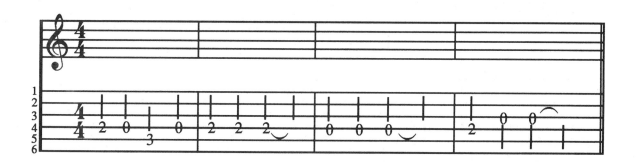

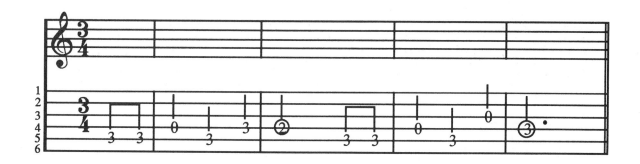

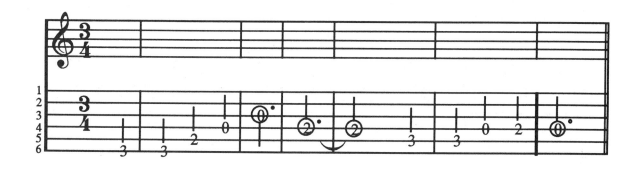

WORK SHEET 12   NAME _____

Notate each pitch given on the fretboard at the left. Examples 1 and 2 have been completed for you. (There are no sharps or flats on this page.)

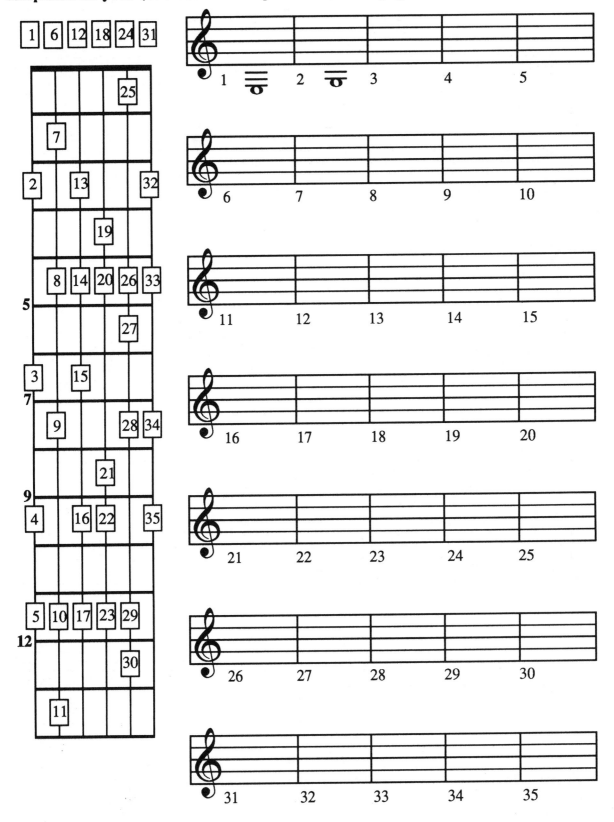

WORK SHEET 13   NAME_____

Sharps and flats have been added. If there are enharmonic pitches, notate both of them.

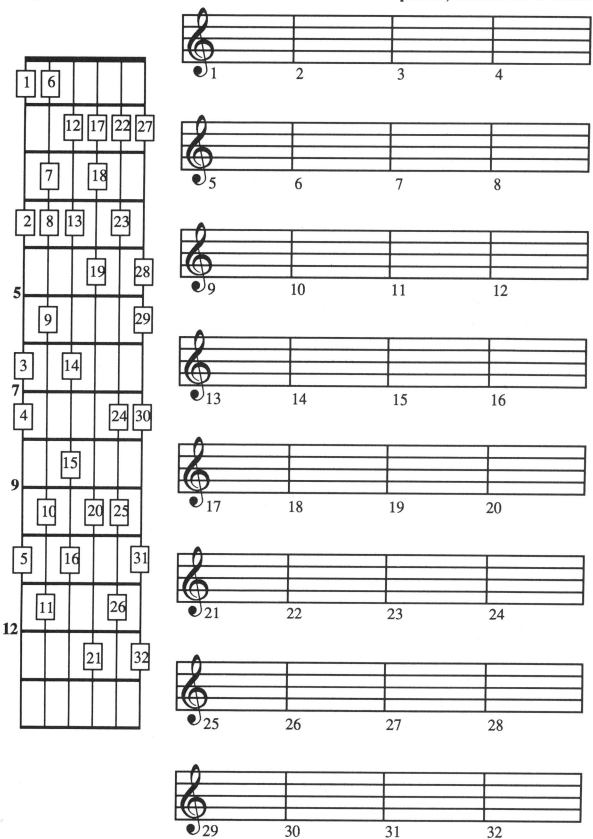

WORK SHEET 14   NAME _____

Transpose the exercises below, using the transposition chart on page 80.

EXAMPLE							
From the key of F:	Fmaj7	Dm7	B♭	C9	F6	Am7♭5	C11
To the key of D:	Dmaj7	Bm7	G	A9	D6	F♯m7♭5	A11

From the key of C: C   Am   Em   F   G11   B7+   G7   G9

To the key of E: ____ ____ ____ ____ ____ ____ ____ ____

To the key of E♭:   ____ ____ ____ ____ ____ ____ ____ ____

From the key of A: F♯m   C♯7   Dmaj7   A   Dsus   Dm   E   E7   E9

To the key of C: ____ ____ ____ ____ ____ ____ ____ ____ ____

To the key of F: ____ ____ ____ ____ ____ ____ ____ ____ ____

From the key of E♭:   E♭   Fm7   B♭7   Cm   A♭   A♭7   Ddim   Gm

To the key of A: ____ ____ ____ ____ ____ ____ ____ ____

To the key of D: ____ ____ ____ ____ ____ ____ ____ ____

From the key of B♭:   F   C   Dm   B♭7   F7   E♭   Gm   Dm   Dm7

To the key of G: ____ ____ ____ ____ ____ ____ ____ ____ ____

To the key of A: ____ ____ ____ ____ ____ ____ ____ ____ ____

From the key of A: B   A   E   D   D7   F♯M7   A7   AMaj7   G♯dim

To the key of B♭:   ____ ____ ____ ____ ____ ____ ____ ____ ____